Wine

Ultimate Wine Handbook — Wine From A-Z, Wine History And Everything Wine

Rutherford Winn

Rutherford Winn

Table Of Contents

Rutherford Winn

Introduction

Congratulations on downloading *"Wine: Everything About Wine from A-Z – Wine History & Everything About Wine."* I thank you for doing so and hope you enjoy it. If you are looking to learn more about wine: the history; evolution; and production of wine, then you have downloaded the right book. The first few chapters dive deep into the history and evolution of wine and how it became a prominent beverage throughout the world. Wine has been used for cultural and religious reasons since the beginning of time. It plays a vital role in religious sacraments throughout the world and is an important part of many countries' economic portfolios.

The production of wine has improved over time, but the same basic ten-step process is used in all wineries around the world. Wine is made by first selecting the wine grapes, then harvesting (which is a crucial step in the process), destemming the grapes, crushing the grapes, pressing the grapes, fermentation (which can be a long process), purifying and refining, preserving, aging, and finally bottling. It is a process that has been improved upon over time and depending on the winery, some or all processes are still completed by hand.

Inside, the first three chapters I will discuss the introduction of wine throughout history, how it was introduced to new countries, what it was used for and the process of producing wine in detail. I will walk through the entire production process from picking the wine grapes to fermentation and aging. I will also discuss some modern versus older techniques and the advantages and disadvantages of each. Some of those older techniques are still used by modern winemakers today, and I will explain why those winemakers may choose to do so. In Chapter 4, I will talk in depth about what specifically makes a good wine, such as the soil, climate, and harvesting. Then, in Chapter 5, I will review the top wine producing countries in the world and in Chapter 6, I will talk about the cost of wine, the different categories of wine based on price and quality and finally, I will review why some wines are more expensive than others.

Once you have an understanding of the history of wine and the production process, the last few chapters will talk more about the culture of wine today such as how to read a wine label, how to properly taste wine, and how to pair it with foods. In Chapter 8, I will teach you how to truly indulge in wine and learn how to pick up on the different flavors and smells. Finally, in Chapter 9, I will review some common food pairings.

There are plenty of books on this subject on the market, so thank you for choosing this one. I hope that you find the information interesting and as useful as possible. Please enjoy!

Rutherford Winn

Chapter 1

Introduction To Wine

Wine is an alcoholic beverage that is a unique experience for everyone. These experiences are based on culture and religion, and also include those interested in the craft of producing wine. Most people that drink wine enjoy it because it tends to take them to another place. It allows them to connect with other regions and environments. It also allows people to have different varieties depending on the mood that they are in. There are so many different flavors to choose from that there is something for everyone.

Wine is a different type of alcoholic beverage than others because it encompasses both a sweet and an acidic taste to balance out the flavor. Although different wines can be sweeter or harsher, they all encompass both. Wines will also have fruity tastes based on the grapes used and how long they ferment. The tannins will contribute to the bitterness which will help determine how sweet or unsweet the wine is as well.

Another important aspect of wine is the smell. The aroma of wine enriches the taste, so it is important that you learn how to drink wine appropriately. Wine's character is first released through smell and then through taste. Therefore, when you first pour a glass of wine, swirl the wine around in your glass as you smell the aroma coming from the glass. You should be able to smell the different fruits, herbs, spices, etc. used in the production of the wine. Smell and swirl your wine a few different times before you take the first drink of wine. Then taste the wine with small sips. Do not gulp your wine, simply take small sips and hold it in your mouth for a good five to ten seconds so that you are able to absorb the taste. Once you swallow, you will then get a distinct aftertaste, which will taste a little bit better than the actual wine itself. Continue to sip on your wine slowly to appreciate the taste, smell, and sensation. I will go into more detail on how to drink wine in Chapter 8.

Wine is made from fermented grapes or other similar fruits. Although wine can be made from other fruits, most wines are made from wine grapes. During fermentation, the sugar from the grapes is turned into alcohol and the yeast gives the wine its flavor. The different varieties of grapes and yeast in the grapes are what changes the taste of the wine.

Wine has been produced for many years. In fact, traces of winemaking have been found in numerous countries throughout history. Archeologists have found evidence of 8,000-year old jars with wine residue in the country of Georgia; a 6,100-year old winery was discovered in Armenia; and 9,000-year old pottery jars have been found in China. Wine has been used throughout history for a variety of reasons and the craft only continues to thrive for the perfect glass of wine.

Wine is made from one or more varieties of grape species. There is a difference in the type of grapes used to make wine. Wine grapes are very different than the table grapes that we eat. Wine grapes are smaller in size, have more seeds, and are much sweeter in taste. There is also a multitude of species of grapes. However, most wines are made from vitis vinifera (red, white, and rose grapes). These grapes can be grown in any climate, which make them viable candidates all over the world. Their natural sugars also allow for natural yeasts, which change into alcohol during fermentation. One of the most common wine grapes is the Cabernet Sauvignon. Some of the major grape production countries in the world include South America, Austria, Mexico, and many eastern countries. There are over 10,000 grape varieties, but only a few are used for commercial use. For wine production, approximately 130 varieties are used. Generally speaking, if one variety of grape is used as the predominant grape in the making of the wine, the result is a varietal wine as opposed to a blended wine. The quality of the wine will closely relate to the soil and climate associated with where the grapes are grown, as well as the winemaking techniques. Grape varieties have different characteristics such as color, skin thickness, acidity levels, the size of the grapes, etc. There are two main wine grape categories: red and white grapes.

The most popular winemaking grapes used are:

Chardonnay: A white grape that is used to make one of the most famous wines in the world. It is also used to make champagne, which is the most famous dessert wine in the world. This grape takes a light green tint and is the fifth most planted grape variety. France is known as its origin. It is produced in large quantities in the United States, New Zealand, South Africa, and Italy.

Merlot: A red grape that is used to make Cabernet Sauvignon. It is the most popular grape variety in France and the second most widely planted grape in the world. It is also popular in Italy, the United States, Romania, Australia, Argentina, Bulgaria, Canada, Chile, Greece, New Zealand, South Africa, Switzerland, Croatia, Hungary, Mexico, Slovenia, and other countries. Merlot wines are often served at lunch or dinner.

Pinotage: A red grape that is a crossbreed of pinot noir and cinsault grapes. These grapes originated in South Africa but are also grown in Brazil, Canada, New Zealand, Israel, the United States, and Zimbabwe. This grape gives the wine a fruity taste, but can come in a range of styles from light-bodied to full-bodied.

Sangiovese: A red grape based out of Italy and most widely used in Chianti, Vino Nobile di Montepulciano, Rosso di Montepulciano, Morellino, etc. There are multiple varieties of the Sangiovese grape used to make these wines. This grape is relatively high in acid and tannins and has a strong fruity taste and smell.

Shiraz or Syrah: A dark red grape variety that is used to produce red wine. The climate determines the wine flavoring that the grape is produced in. For a sweeter wine it is grown in a warmer climate and for a spicier/peppery flavor, it is grown in cooler climates. These grapes are grown in France, Chile, South Africa, New Zealand, and the United States.

Zinfandel: A dark red/black grape that produces a red wine with a berry fruit flavor when grown in cooler areas and a blackberry with pepper flavor when produced in warmer areas. One of the most popular rosé wines sold is the White Zinfandel.

Introduction to the Production of Wine

Wine production has not changed much since the beginning of time, with the exception of machinery replacing humans. The ability to use machines for pressing grapes, funneling the juice, and bottling, means that the process can become more streamlined and enhance the quality of wine. However, some wineries do not agree with this method and continue to do most of the work by hand.

Wine is only produced once a year because of the length of time it takes for wine grapes to ripen. However, winemakers also have to take into consideration how long it takes the yeast to regulate and how long the fermentation process will take. Winemaking includes four main steps: harvesting and crushing; fermenting; aging; and packaging. Later in this book, we will dive into more detail about the production of wine.

Each wine bottle will have the year the wine was made, which is called the vintage year, if 95% of the wine was made from grapes harvested in that particular year (this may vary by country). This year includes when the grapes were picked and when the wine was produced. Vintage stands for winemaking age. Harvesting for wine grapes takes place from August to September for the northern hemisphere and February to April for the southern hemisphere. If a wine bottle does not have a vintage date, then the wine does not meet the vintage percentage requirements.

On occasion, a non-vintage wine will be made. This is a blend of several different years of wine such as Champagne. These bottles of wine will have the letters "NV" on the bottom instead of a vintage year, indicating it is non-vintage.

As mentioned briefly above, varietal wine is a wine made with one type of grape. For example, Riesling is made with Riesling grapes. Every country has a unique set of rules related to how much variety needs to be included in wine to be labeled single-varietal wine. To be labeled as a single-varietal wine, 75% of the wine must be made from one kind of grape in the United States (except for Oregon, which requires 90%), Chile, South Africa, Australia, and Greece. In Argentina, 80% of the wine must be made from one type of grape. In Italy, France, Germany, Austria, Portugal, Spain, and New Zealand, 85% of the wine needs to be made from one type of grape.

Wine blends are popular because they are made with several different grape varieties (it is important to note that blends are mixed after fermentation). Field blends are made when the grapes are blended before fermentation. Some famous wine blends include Champagne, Red Bordeaux, White Bordeaux, Port, and Cava.

There is a difference in how red and white wines are made. Red wine is made directly from the grapes while white wine is made from the grape juice. There are also wines, such as blush wines, that are made from red grape skins with limited contact to the juice.

Red grapes contain a green mushy inside, but they have a red skin on the outside. During the winemaking process, the juice from the inside and the skin on the outside play a major role in the color, flavor, and tannins in the final wine product. After the grapes are crushed, a fermentation process requires the crushed grapes to sit in a container for a period of time. During this process, the juice sinks, while the skins rise to the top forming a top layer. Typically, the skin will be mixed back in with the fermenting juice, this is called "must." After fermentation, the wine is taken from the container where it must be clarified and then moved into an oak barrel for aging. Once it is ready, it is then packaged into bottles for labeling and sale.

White grapes will go straight to crushing after picking. The skins are separated from the juice, which is entirely different than the red grape process. Occasionally, winemakers will adjust the acid or sugar levels of the white grape juice for fermentation. Then yeast is added so that alcohol can be made during fermentation. After fermentation, filtering and some sweetening may need to be done to get the desired flavor. White wine processing is different than red in that you have to add a lot of manual processing to get the desired flavor and color. After fermentation and sweetening, the wine is ready for aging. It is moved to an oak barrel for the aging process. After the aging process, it is bottled, labeled, and made available for sale.

How Wines Are Named

Most wines get their name from the grape variety they are produced from or the region in the world where the wine is made. More often than not the name comes from where the wine is made. However, each region in the world has their own rules and, depending on if it is old wine or new wine, it may also follow a different logic. This is why some wines have very similar tastes.

Most of the wines made in the "Old World" are and were named after their region because winemakers feel and have felt that where the wine is made has as much to do with the wine as the wine grape itself. Terroir is an old French term that means "sense of place." Winemakers believed that it was important to include the terroir in the wine name because it is what gives the wine its character and unique taste and smell. For example, Cabernet Sauvignon produced in Bordeaux will taste much different than that made in Italy. The wine grapes, although similar, have very different characteristics that determine the characteristics of the terroir (the moon cycles, soil, rain, and climate of the region). Think about fruits grown in various parts of the world, they all taste different depending on where they are grown. The same is true for wine grapes, which is why they wine will taste different even though it is the same grape. The term terroir is just a fancy term for the land, climate, and natural environment that gives the wine grape its distinctive character.

Whereas Old World wine is named after its region, most "New World" regions name their wine after the grape variety. For example, Riesling grapes are used to make

Riesling wine. This is the simplest form of naming wine and you know exactly what type of wine you are drinking. If the wine is varietal wine, the wine is named after the principal grape used. Each country has laws requiring a minimum percentage of grapes that wine must contain to name itself by a grape. This ensures that the names are accurate. Most varietal wines do not actually indicate the other grapes that are used in the wines, so you only know the primary grape used to make the wine by its name. However, some varietals are made 100% of the wine grape it is named after.

Non-Grape Wines

As mentioned above there are wines that are made from fruits other than grapes. While the remainder of this book will focus on grape wines, it is useful and interesting to learn a bit about the other types of wine that are available. For those who are very interested in grape wines, they might wish to explore other kinds of wine as well.

Fruit wines are made by fermenting different kinds of fruit, and often also adding flavors from flowers and herbs as well. Historically fruit wines have been popular with people who make homemade wine and in areas with cooler climates such as Scandinavia and North America. Fruit wines are made in some warmer countries too, though; in India, Africa, and the Philippines, for example, fruit wine is made from bananas. Common fruit wines include elderberry wine, dandelion wine, and elder blow wine (made from elderberry flowers).

The traditional definition of "wine" is fermented grape juice, so most countries or regions require that fruit wines are labeled so as to clearly indicate that the beverages are not made from grapes. In fact, in the European Union, the legal definition of wine is fermented grape juice, so fruit wine producers are legally required to name their beverages so as to make it clear that they are not grape wine. Fruit wines are usually named after their main fruit ingredient, such as elderberry wine or plum wine. In the United Kingdom, "country wine" is the common name for fruit wine, but in British legislation, it is referred to as "made-wine."

Most berries and fruits can be used in the production of wine; as long as a plant can be fermented, it can produce wine. Due to the fact that there are few fruits other than grapes that have the proper balance of acid, sugar, salts to feed yeast, tannin, and water that are required to produce a drinkable wine, fruit wine producers have learned to add ingredients that will allow for those ingredients to be present in the final product. Sugar or honey are common additives as they make the fruit wines more palatable and help to raise the alcoholic content since sucrose converts to alcohol during the fermentation process. This process of adding sugar to increase the alcohol in the beverage is called chaptalization. If too much natural sugar is present, or if too much has been added, then water or a combination of acid (usually from lime, lemon, or vinegar) can be added to reduce the sugar content.

Many of the fruits that are used in fruit wines have a high natural acid content, which would prevent the final product from being pleasant-tasting if not tempered with an additive. This is particularly true of cherries, strawberries, raspberries, and pineapples. As with high sugar content, when there is too much acid water can be added to reduce the acidity prior to fermentation. This has the side effect of diluting or reducing the fruit flavor, which can be compensated for by adding sugar or another sweetening agent after fermentation. When sugar is added after the fermentation process, it is called a back-sweetener.

Fruits used to produce fruit wines also tend to lack the natural yeast nutrients that are needed to create or maintain fermentation. Winemakers deal with this problem by adding commercially-available phosphorus, nitrogen, and potassium.

For the most part, fruit wines do not improve with age after bottling, unlikely many of their grape counterparts. Fruit wines are generally best if drank within a year of being bottled.

<u>Types of Fruit Wines</u>

Plum Wine

Plum wine, also known as plum liquor, is popular in Korea and Japan, and to a lesser extent in China where it is called meiju. Plum wine is produced from distilled liquor that has been soaked with plums; as a result, the alcoholic content is higher than most fruit wines.

In Japan, a sweet and smooth plum wine called umeshu is made by steeping green plums in a clear liquor called shōchū. In Korea, a wine similar to the Japanese shōchū is made, which is called maesil. In both Japan and Korea, the plum wines are sold with whole prune fruits placed in the bottle.

Plum wine is also produced in Taiwan, where it is called wumeijiu. This smoked plum liquor is made by mixing two plum liquors, *prunus mume* and *prunus salicina*, with oolong tea liquor.

Outside of Asia, the only region that produced plum wine to any significant degree was in the north Cotswolds of Britain, which traditionally made a plum jerkum using plums in a similar way to how apples are used to produce cider. The popularity of this drink has waned in recent years, however.

Pineapple Wine

Pineapple wine is made from the juice of pineapples; none of the pineapple flesh is used. The pineapple juice is fermented in temperature-controlled vats, and the fermentation process is halted at a near-dryness level. Pineapple wine is a dry, soft wine with a strong pineapple bouquet. This type of wine is very popular in Thailand and other Southeast Asian countries. In many of these countries, it is made using traditional practices and is not produced at a commercial level or even made available commercially.

Pineapple wine is also produced in some countries outside of Southeast Asia. In Japan, several types of pineapple wine are made from local produce. In Mexico, pineapple wine is called Tepache and is highly popular. More commercial examples include Hawaii's Maui's Winery and Nigeria's Jacobs Wines, which was the first African pineapple winery. The Vinicola Del Norte winery in the Dominican Republic also produces a commercially available pineapple wine. Commercial products tend to have an alcohol level in the range of 10% to 12%, which traditional beverages can have an even higher alcoholic content.

Dandelion Wine

Dandelion wine is made from combining dandelion petals with sugar, and then adding an acid (such as lime or lemon juice) and wine-making chemicals like sodium metabisulfite. For the most part dandelion wines are made on a local, homemade level; there are very few commercial dandelion wine products. The dandelion wines that are commercially available are all made at wineries in the United States, including in New Jersey, Ohio, Montana, and North Dakota.

Rose Hip Wine

Rose hip wine can be made from dried or fresh rose hips. The rose hips are fermented in syrup, with yeast and a citric acid added to create an extract. This technique for making fruit wine is rare and is used in only a few other fruit wines in addition to rose hip wine. Other types of fruit wine made with this technique include hawthorn, blackthorn (sloe), and rowan wines.

Red currant or White currant Wine

Both red currant and white currant wines are produced primarily in northern areas where the climate is cool, and it is difficult to grow wine-quality grapes. Red currants and white currants are some of the few fruits that have a natural chemical balance, which makes the production of wine easy and does not require the addition of other substances other than a small amount of honey or sugar.

Cherry Wine

Tart cherries are most commonly used in the production of cherry wine, as they have the necessary acid levels to produce a good fruit wine. Michigan is the leading region in the United States for the production of tart cherries, and as a result, there are several Michigan winemakers who produce various types of cherry wine, including cherry-grape blends and spiced cherry wines.

A fortified cherry wine called Cherry Kijafa is produced in Denmark; this wine has an alcoholic content of 16%. Kijafa is often exported to other countries in Europe and to North America.

Banana Wine

Banana wine is a different beverage than banana beer, which is a traditional drink of East Africa. Banana wine is produced by fermenting ripe bananas that have been peeled and mashed. Water is added to dilute the otherwise thick mash, and wine yeast and sugar are added to assist the fermentation process. While there are other some commercial producers, including in Tanzania, for the most part, banana wine is produced on a small scale by home winemakers. Since the early 2000s, the Philippine government has been attempting to expand its banana wine industry. India has actually produced some award-winning banana wines and has done some excellent research into techniques for expanding production of banana wine. Commercial brands of banana wine include Malkia, which is sweet and clear with an alcohol content of 11%, and Meru, which is clear and dry and also has an 11% alcohol content.

Lychee Wine

Lychee wine is a traditional Chinese dessert wine made entirely with lychee fruit. The wine is full-bodied, with a golden color and a sweet, rich taste. Lychee wine is usually served cold with food, and pairs best with Asian cuisine including shellfish. It can also be paired with other liquors as a cocktail mixer.

Chapter 2

The Evolution And History Of Wine

Wine has been used and improved upon from as far back as 10,000 B.C. Grapes and grapevines have been around for even longer, although archeology has not been able to confirm for how long. Archaeologists believe that humans collected berries to enjoy their sweet flavor and likely discovered "wine" by allowing some berries to sit for a few days and ferment. It has been a part of the culture in many countries as expansion and growth became prominent. It is believed that the earliest known form of wine was made from honey or berries. If this is the case, a tradition of wine has been around for over 10,000 years, because archaeologists found pottery from the 8,000 B.C. period that resembled this substance. Chemical analysis found a fermented drink substance on pottery from this time period, indicating that a fermented beverage with rice, honey, grapes, and berries were made. Around 10,000 to 8,000 B.C., humans switched from a nomadic lifestyle to a more sedentary one, which is likely what led to the development of agriculture and organized wine production rather than the accidental or "one-off" productions of earlier humans.

The origin of wine is based mainly around religious worship and predates any written history. The Greeks worshiped both Dionysus and Bacchus, who were gods of harvesting and winemaking. The Romans continued this religious sanction by worshipping the same gods. Jewish religious practices involved drinking ritual wine, and this has been even more prominent in the Christian Church, more specifically Catholicism. While Islam did forbid the consumption or production of wine, during the Golden Age of Islam (from the 8th to 13th centuries, when science, economics, and math flourished in the Islamic culture), there were Islamic scientists who produced wine for industrial and medicinal purposes, including the creation of perfumes. In fact, the Uyghurs (a distinct ethnic group) of Turkey were primarily responsible for reestablishing viticulture in China, starting in the Tang dynasty in the 7th century A.D. From what we have learned, the origins of wine have an ancient past dating back to Egypt, Phoenicia, Greece, China, and the Roman Empire.

Many cultures have a mythology relating to the cultivation of grapevines and the production of wine. In Christianity and Judaism, for example, wine production is first mentioned in Genesis, when Noah gets drunk and exposes himself to his sons after the Great Flood. In Greek mythology, as mentioned above, the Greek god Dionysus was heavily involved with wine production (and consumption). It was claimed that as a child, Dionysus discovered viticulture at Mount Nysa. He eventually taught the practice of wine production to the people of central Anatolia, and as a result was rewarded by becoming the god of wine.

According to Persian legend, a mythological figure named King Jamshid was believed to have banished one of the women from his harem. Despondent from being banished, the woman attempted to commit suicide by drinking a jar that contained the remnants of spoiled grapes, which were thought to be poisonous as a result of the fermentation.

Upon drinking the fermented juice, she felt much happier and took her discovery to King Jamshid. The King was apparently so happy with the new drink that he took the woman back into his harem and made a decree that all of the grapes grown in Persepolis were to be used for winemaking.

Evidence of wine production has been found in locations in Georgia (~6,000 B.C.), Iran (~5,000 B.C.), Greece (~4500 B.C.), and Armenia. The oldest known winery was founded in Ancient Armenia in 4,100 B.C. Inside a cave a wine press was found along with fermentation and storage vessels. Around the cave, the explorers found drinking cups and old grape vines with skins and seeds from the grapes. The equipment was tested to find out if the chemicals were in fact wine residue. The test revealed traces of malvidin, which is responsible for the pigment in red wine. Archaeologists believe that the fact that wine production was so well-developed by 4,000 B.C. suggests that the ability and knowledge probably had been around for quite some time prior to that; so while this is the earliest *known* winery, it is very likely that it is not the first or even one of the earliest wineries. What is particularly interesting about this discovery is that the seeds found in the cave were from the species *Vitis vinifera*, which is still used today in wine production. While technology and production tools have advanced significantly since the first wine production attempts, the original grapevine species still holds up.

Wine making also began in Mesopotamia and areas around the Caspian Sea between 6,000 and 4,000 B.C. At this time, wine was the preferred drink by royalty and priests. The Egyptians were the first culture to actually document the process they used for winemaking. Several caves, clay tablets, and burial chambers have been found by archeologists with descriptions of harvesting grapes and the process they used to make the wine.

Based on other history that we are aware of, the Pharaohs in Egypt began making their own wine using red grapes for use during ceremonies because of its resemblance to blood. This became a common practice and it was the Phoenicians that began the tradition of wine throughout the world in 3,100 B.C. Historians believe the industry of wine began during an Egypt and Canaan trade during the Early Bronze Age. Shedeh was the most ritualistic drink in ancient Egypt, which was a red wine. However, five clay containers are known to have been found in Tutankhamun's tomb by archaeologists. Residue examined found it to be white wine. This suggests that white wine was available during this time period, but it just was not as prominent as red wine. Scenes of winemaking found on tomb walls, which lists of offerings that included wines, clearly show that wine was widely produced by the Egyptians during this period. By 2600 B.C., wines had become so central to Egyptian culture that five types of wine were considered as a proper and complete set of provisions for those entering the afterlife.

In 1700 B.C., archaeologists discovered a large 3,700-year-old cellar in Northern Israel in the location of the palace of the rulers of Tel Kabri. Inside the cellar, archeologists would discover how popular wine was there as well. They found roughly 40 Canaanite storage jars inside this cellar. This means that they could store nearly 2,000 liters of wine! The palace was destroyed during a conflict, leveling what we now know was a wine cellar. Archeologists tested the jars to find out if in fact wine had been inside the jars. Both tartaric and syringic acid were found in these jars. Both were commonly used in winemaking as well as honey, mint, cinnamon, and other ingredients used in ancient Egyptian wines.

Between 1200 B.C. and 539 B.C., the Phoenicians began to trade across the Mediterranean into North Africa, Greece, Italy, and other areas of Europe They were well known for their trading abilities and owned much of the prosperity. Wine was just one of their trades, but it did help to introduce wine to other parts of the world. Phoenicians were instrumental in the distribution of wine. Their knowledge of winemaking techniques, wine grapes, and technology helped the industry to flourish. They played an important role in wine development in Greece and Rome. This was also the around the time the Jewish community began to include wine into their religious ceremonies, which is still a common practice today. Their use of amphoras became necessary as well because more and more areas of the world began using similar clay-like containers for their wine.

The Greeks were the ones who began perfecting the beverage, which made it even more of a commodity and religious/health product. One of the ways in which the Greeks improved wine production was to use partially dehydrated gypsum prior to fermentation and lime afterward, which resulted in reduced acidity of the beverage. Many of the grapes used in wine today are only grown in Greece, and they are identical to those used in ancient Greece; this includes the grapes that are used to produce retsina, a strong and aromatic white wine which is the most popular type of Modern Greek wine. The unique flavor of retsina is believed to have originally resulted from the ancient Greeks' practice of lining wine jugs with resin from trees. Wine played a very important role in ancient Greek culture; in fact, they named a god, Dionysus, after wine. The ancient Greeks celebrated wine with a festival called "Feast of the Wine," which celebrated the "Month of the New Wine."

The earliest known reference to a variety of wine that had been given a specific name is from the 7th century B.C. when the poet Alcman wrote praises of a wine called Dénthis. A wine called Chian was the first named red wine (known to the Greeks as "black wine"). Another popular Greek wine was Coan, from the island of Kos, which was mixed with ocean water to create a salty beverage. Wines from Lesbos and Lemnos were also very popular. In fact,

Lemnió, a red wine with a bouquet of thyme and oregano, produced on Lemnos, is still produced today and is the oldest known type of wine in cultivation.

As the Greeks would conquer a new territory, they would bring wine and grape vines along with them, forming a new tradition in that area of the world. Wine became a staple in the Greek tradition in 800 B.C. Although China was actually credited for the first red wine, Greeks saw red wine as black wine. Different cultures meant that wines were characterized differently. The Greeks ultimately saw wine as a way to seek economic growth and stability.

While archaeologists have discovered evidence of production in China of wine-like beverages from native mountain grapes as far back as the 2nd millennia B.C., wine was not predominant in China until around the 2nd century B.C. Instead, the Chinese focused primarily on the production of drinks produced from rice, millet, and other grains. In the 2nd century B.C., trade with the Greeks brought viticulture to Central Asia and eventually China. However, the consumption of wine was primarily for the imperial family and its court until the 10th century A.D. when it spread to the gentry. Grape wine never became as popular in China as rice wine, however; even today, rice wine is consumed at much higher levels than grape wine.

Lebanon is one of the oldest wine production sites in the world. The Phoenicians were instrumental in bringing wine to this portion of the Middle East. However, after the Muslims conquered much of the territory in the 7th and 8th centuries, alcohol was prohibited by them. It seems that the production of wine continued, but it was only used for private and social gatherings. The religious sacrament was another use for wine during this time by Egyptian Jews throughout the Eastern Mediterranean.

Once Rome conquered Greece in 146 B.C., they took wine on as their own, creating their own god of wine, Bacchus. The rise of the Roman Empire played an integral part in winemaking. They made wine a staple in their heritage and built upon what the Greeks did and cultivated new methods. Wine was a daily drink available to everyone. In fact, the Romans were the first to develop social norms for drunkenness and alcoholism. Wine laws had to be passed because of an increase in alcoholism. Evidence suggests that the popularity and availability of wine had increased so much within the Roman Empire by the first century that this was when widespread alcoholism and drunkenness began to be a problem, with the peak of the problem occurring in the first century A.D. This led then-Emperor Domitian to pass laws that banned the planting of any new vineyards in Italy itself, and removing many of the vineyards in the Roman provinces. While these laws were largely ignored by the Roman people, they remained on the books until repealed by Emperor Probus in 280 A.D.

Roman winemaking was popular and used very distinct processes. The wine was very alcoholic, and the style of wines grew. White wine was the most highly regarded, but other wines were available to the Romans. Grapevines spread throughout the area and become popular in France, Germany, Spain, Portugal, and Italy; in fact, virtually all of Western Europe's wine-producing regions of today were established during Rome's Imperial era. The popularity of wine blossomed due to the Romans. Wine was used for medical purposes, religious purposes, and recreational purposes. Winemaking technology flourished under the Roman Empire, along with the creation of wine storage rooms for aging and bottling apparatuses. New grape varieties and blends were created along with new cultivation techniques.

The Romans built wine storage rooms to face north, since they believed that the northern "quarter" was constant and not subject to change, and so would result in more stable wines. They also developed smokehouses (called "fumaria") that were used to speed up or mimic the aging process. The Romans began to incorporate storage vessels from other cultures into their wine production, including barrels from the Gauls and glass bottles from the Syrians; these began to compete with the traditional terracotta amphoras for the storage and shipping of Roman wine. After the Greeks invented the screw, Roman winemakers also began to use wine presses for their wine production.

It was the Romans who introduced the first naming system for wine, as different regions began to develop reputations for their high-quality wines. The white wine Falernian was produced in the Latian (now Latium)-Campanian border area, and was popular because of its high alcohol content of 15% or higher. Falernian wine was actually divided into three categories of its own: Caucinian, from the highest slopes of the region, Faustian from the center of the region, and generic Falernian from the plains and lower slopes. Other popular wines included Alban, a sweet wine from the Alban Hills; and Caecuban, a strong, smooth wine from the ager Caecubus region in what is now known as the Pontine Marshes.

Wine mixed with minerals and herbs was used for medicinal purposes. The upper classes believed that dissolving pearls in wine would lead to better health. Cleopatra is believed to have been the origin of this belief, having told Antony that she would "drink the value of a province" in a cup of wine and then adding an expensive pearl to her drink. When Emperor Augustus rose to power, Setinum wine was declared to be the imperial wine because it did not give Augustus indigestion.

In 380 A.C., the Roman Empire adopted Catholicism and Christianity and wine became an important part of the religious sacrament. Catholics used wine as a part of their mass celebrations and began to focus on the cultivation and production of wine. The use of wine in religious sacraments is still true today for Catholics. Monks began working as vintners in Italy and France, perfecting the winemaking process. Catholicism began to grow in France, taking wine there as well. In fact, when the Roman Empire fell in the 5th century A.D., the Roman Catholic Church was the only remaining stable social structure of that culture, and it was largely thanks to the church that the Roman techniques for grape growing and winemaking were preserved in history.

The oldest known surviving bottle of wine, called the Speyer wine bottle, belonged to a Roman nobleman. This bottle is dated to 325 or 350 A.D.

Thanks to the need for the use of wine in Catholic Mass, the Benedictine monks eventually became one of the most prevalent wine producers in Germany and France, and the Cistericans, Carthusians, Carmelites, and Templars also produced their fair share. The Benedictines had vineyards in Champagne, Bordeaux, and Burgundy in France, and in the German regions of Franconia and Rheingau. In 1435, a member of the Holy Roman high nobility named Count John IV of Katzenelnbogen planted the first Riesling grapes. The monks in the surrounding area quickly developed an industry around Riesling, eventually producing sufficient amounts that the wine could be shipped throughout Europe for secular and religious use.

While wine had previously been restricted primarily to the upper classes in Europe because of its reduced availability and therefore higher expense, by the 1400s wine had become so prevalent that it was consumed by the majority of the population. Wine was served at virtually every meal, in every household. Most wines were still kept in barrels, and because of this they did not age well, and were usually drunk while still fairly young.

Between 1492 and 1600, wine was brought to the New World through Mexico and Brazil by Spanish Conquistadors. The indigenous peoples of the Americas had been producing alcoholic beverages for centuries, using crops such as potatoes, maize, quinoa, tree fruits, and strawberries as a base. However, despite the fact that there were some native grape species in the Americas, the indigenous peoples did not ferment the grapes and did not make grape wine until wine was introduced by the Conquistadors.

South Americans adapted to wine, and it spread like wildfire, creating Spanish wine. The cultivation of vines became prominent as the Spanish took over Latin America. The main reason for this was the religious rituals that wine had in Catholicism. Immigrants brought wine grapes from France, Italy and Germany, which drastically improved wine production. The first attempts to grow grape vines in the Americas occurred on the island of Hispaniola after Columbus' second voyage in 1494. However, in the 16th century, the Spanish commercial production of wine began to decline a bit due to the competitive nature of the production of the immigrant wine. Therefore, the Spanish King Ferdinand II of Aragon required that Hispaniola stopped producing other wines because of its effect on their own wine production. In 1524 however, Hernán Cortés, the conqueror of Mexico, wanted to promote the establishment of vineyards in the country and made it a requirement that if Spanish settlers wanted to acquire land in Mexico, they must plant grapes on their lands.

Peru's first foray into grape-growing was by two individuals named Francisco de Carabantes and Barolome de Terrazas in the 1540s. De Carabantes managed to establish vineyards in the Ica region, and those vines were later introduced into Argentina and Chile.

New World wine was not considered as good quality as other wine for quite some time, but in the 20th century, it gained respect.

In 1543, three Portuguese missionaries sailed to Japan, taking wine with them. Six years later, Saint Francis Xavier took wine to Japan for the feudal lords of Kyushu as gifts. Around this same time, imported European wine was brought into the population, and this led to the conversion of over 100,000 Japanese citizens to Catholicism.

In 1587, Toyotomi Hideyoshi reunified Japan, banning Christianity. Persecution of Christians took place until Western missionaries arrived in the 19th century. Nearly 300 years later, grapevines were planted, embracing wine and the Western culture during the Meiji restoration. Emperor Meiji helped unify Japan and restore the government. Restoration in the country led to domestic wine production and techniques.

Chile's first winery was established in 1554 when Spanish Conquistadors and missionaries traveled from Mexico and other areas from the North. Francisco de Aguirre planted the very first vines. Initially, most wines were imported until about the 18th century. Chile is known for its sweet wines and was extremely successful at introducing Cabernet Sauvignon, Merlot, and Carmenere in the 19th Century. In 1556, the Spanish missionaries traveled from Chile to Argentina, planting grapes for the first time. Juan Cedron established the first vineyard in Argentina with cuttings from Chile. Argentina is now the fifth largest producer of wine.

When grapes were first grown in the Americas, one of the most common varieties was the Mission grape, a black grape. This grape was called Negra peruana in Peru, which was the source of the most common grape in Chile, the País. The País was eventually introduced into Argentina, where it was known as Criolla chica. While the original source grape, the Mission, is believed to have come from Spain, it may also have come from Italy as it closely resembles the Mónica grape which was first grown in Sardinia and then Spain.

In the 1500s and 1600s Peru was the most predominant wine-producing region, and in particular the regions of Pisco and Ica. Chile also had a relatively strong wine production industry, and Paraguay began to develop as a wine-making region in the late 1500s.

In 1595 the Spanish King attempted to ban the establishment of vineyards in the Americas, but for the most part, this order was ignored by the population. The ban's intention was to protect the Spanish wine exportation to the Americas, but by that point, domestic wines (and in particular Peruvian wines) were so popular that the ban had little effect. Further attempts to protect Spanish wine sales were attempted by the Spanish Crown in 1614 and 1615, when it banned the exportation of Peruvian wine to Panama and Guatemala, respectively. Again, these bans were largely ignored, and there was little actual enforcement of the bans.

In fact, the growth of Bolivia to become the largest city in the Americas in the 1600s, and of Lima which was one of the most important political centers in South America at the time, served to further increase the popularity of Peruvian wines as the populations largely demanded domestic wines. By the late 17th century Peruvian and Chilean wines were so popular that Paraguay determined that it could not compete in the market; instead, it moved to growing tobacco and other crops, and by the 18th century Paraguay had virtually stopped producing wine.

Peru's lead over the wine market ceased in 1687 when an earthquake struck the whole southern coast of the country, destroying most of the vineyards and wine cellars in the Pisco and Ica regions. While the Jesuits in Peru continued to produce wine to some degree, the 1767 suppression of the Society of Jesus led to their vineyards being auctioned to non-Jesuit owners who did not have the same level of expertise, leading to an even further decline of Peruvian wine production. By the late 1700s, wine production in Peru had decreased so significantly that it was required to import wine from Chile.

Between 1562 and 1564, wine was made for the first time in North America by French Huguenots in Jacksonville, Florida. Native grapes were used instead of those brought from Europe. Unfortunately, Huguenots did not think the wine was of good quality because of the grapes used. The promotion of wine in America would continue later.

Quebec City, Canada was permanently founded by Samuel de Champlain in 1608. He planted local grapes to begin cultivating wine in this area. Unfortunately, they did not resist water very well, but production began nonetheless. Imports of wine began to take place over the years as well.

In 1619, the French began importing French grapevines to Virginia to start cultivating wine there as well. It took many years before the use of native vineyards would be successful, but eventually, the Eastern Seaboard began to see winemaking take off. By 1787, the United States saw its first official commercial winery in Pennsylvania, created by Pierre Legaux.

New Zealand, Australia, and South Africa were late to the wine game, and even today are still considered New World producers. South Africa successfully produced its first wine from French Muscadel grapes in 1659, after unsuccessful attempts in 1654. The Dutch East India Company colonized in South Africa and wanted to build a supply station for sailors heading back and forth to Europe. Cape Province (Cape of Good Hope) became the place that would fill this void.

A Spanish missionary, Junipero Serra, traveled from Spain to the New World in 1769 in an effort to spread the gospel. He spent time in Mexico City before moving to San Diego to establish a mission. San Diego would become the region's first home to wine. He helped spread this art throughout California, as well as the art of making wine, with the support of the Franciscan monks who built Sonoma's first winery in 1805.

Thomas Jefferson became the French Prime Minister in 1785. He fell in love with wine as he traveled around France, more specifically with Bordeaux and Burgundy. He took French grape cuttings to Virginia to help wine thrive in the United States.

The First Fleet departed from the United Kingdom in 1787 for Australia. A stop was made in South Africa where grape cuttings from the Cape of Good Hope were brought to the penal colony in Australia for planting. It took some time to perfect the production of wine after failing the first few tries, but in the 1820s wine was finally available for sale domestically.

In 1832, James Busy was appointed as the British Resident of New Zealand. He was considered the father of the Australian wine industry. He took grape cuttings from Australia to New Zealand to establish their first vineyard in 1836.

Until the late 20th century, most wines produced in Australia, New Zealand, and South Africa were consumed only within the countries and were not commercially popular in other areas. Australia did export some wines to the United Kingdom, while New Zealand tended to retain its wines for domestic consumption, and South Africa was separated from the world market for some time due to apartheid.

Today, however, these countries are known for producing high-quality wines, thanks to recent advances in winemaking techniques and technologies.

Between 1848 and 1855, it was known as the Gold Rush in California. Americans seeking prosperity would move west in hopes of finding a better life, along with a taste for good wine. Those on the east coast took vines with them as they migrated westward. California began creating vineyards with grapes mostly indigenous to France, such as the Zinfandel. California is still known for this grape which originated in Croatia.

In the 1830s, the French took control of Algeria. They began replenishing the vineyards that the Phoenicians planted years before. During the 1860s and 1870s, wine production boomed and hit a high point in the 1930s when exportation became a major industry. French winemakers in the Languedoc used much of the wine for blending during this time. However, in 1962, the French ceded, causing wine production to go into a long decline in this area for many years.

Wine production in Europe experienced a significant decline in the late 19th century when an epidemic of phylloxera decimated the European wineries. Phylloxera is an insect pest that feeds on the leaves and roots of grapevines. In addition to the damage suffered by having large numbers of insects eating the plants' roots and leaves, some types of grapevines suffered from deformations on the roots (called "tuberosities" or "nodosities") and fungal infections as a result of phylloxera attacks. These deformations and fungal infections had the effect of girdling the roots of the grapevines, preventing the plants from getting the necessary nutrients and water. As well, phylloxera nymphs would form protective galls (swelling growths) on the undersides of the plants' leaves, further affecting the plants' ability to circulate nutrients and water.

The phylloxera was introduced to Europe as a result of English botanists collecting specimens of American grapevines in the 1850s and bringing those specimens to

England. While most species of North American grapevines were at least somewhat resistant to phylloxera, since phylloxera is native to North America, the European grapevines had never encountered the pest before and had no resistance. The epidemic began in England and then moved outward to Europe, devastating the majority of Europe's vineyards starting in 1863. In 1875, the wine produced in France totaled 84.5 million hectoliters; by 1889, that production had decreased to 23.4 million hectoliters as a result of the plague.

Many different strategies were attempted to fight the phylloxera plague, including placing toads under the plants to draw out the poison, which turned out to be completely ineffective. A strategy that was widely popular was the idea that if European grapevines were hybridized with North American resistant species, this would help the plants to recover and resist the phylloxera. The problem with this strategy was that at the time, North American grapes produced a flavor that was very different than what the European palates preferred, so viviculturalists had to come up with a hybrid that could resist phylloxera and still produce a flavor that was at least similar to the traditional

European wines – not an easy task! Unfortunately for the European wineries, it turned out that the hybrid species, while much hardier than their origin species, were not any more resistant to phylloxera. Today, those species are discouraged, if not banned, throughout Europe, although they are used in some North American wines.

The strategy that eventually ended up being at least moderately successful was grafting the European grapevines species with resistant rootstocks. A rootstock is a part of the plant, usually underground, which can be used to produce new above-ground growth. This strategy was much more effective than the hybridization attempts and was partially responsible for the recovery of European vineyards.

There were some European species of grapevines that survived the phylloxera plague, as they were somehow resistant: the Assyrtiko grape, which grows on the island of Santorini in Greece; and the Juan Garcia grape, which is native to Spain. Other regions of Europe had their grapevines so destroyed that they ended up planting other crops instead; on the island of Mallorca, for example, almonds are now grown instead of grapes.

Today the phylloxera pest still exists, but scientific discoveries and new technology have allowed modern grapevines species to adapt so that phylloxera is only a minor threat that can be easily overcome.

Despite Europe's difficulties with phylloxera, in other areas of the world wine production continued its expansion. Uruguay's National Grape was planted in 1870 by a French Basque immigrant named Don Pascual Harriague, who also planted Tannat vines. His intention was to bring wine alive in this area of the world, which eventually became a staple.

Chilean wine also continued to thrive, and in fact began to improve thanks to modernization. In 1851, a Chilean winemaker named Silvestre Ochagavia imported cuttings of French and other grape varieties; these varieties included Pinot noir, Cabernet Sauvignon, Merlot, Cot, Riesling, and Semillon. Other winemakers quickly followed suit, and by the 1870s the Chilean wine industry was one the most successful industries in Chile.

Argentina experienced a significant wine boom in the 19th and early 20th centuries, and the country eventually became the fifth highest-producing wine region in the world and the highest in Latin America. In 1885 the Buenos Aires-

Menodoza railroad allowed trade to expand significantly while also lowering trading costs, which allowed for the development of vineyards in the Mendoza region of Argentina. Around that same time, there was a substantial immigration to Argentina from southern Europe, which both increased the demand for wine and introduced Old World expertise to the country's wine industry. By 1910 Argentina had more vineyards than Chile and a more modern wine industry.

Between 1980 and 2013, the Chinese economy boomed under the Deng Xiaoping regime. He began importing French wine, which brought French immigrants who partnered to build new wineries around the country. This caused China's middle and upper-class population to grow exponentially. China became one of the world's largest producers and consumers of wine. Today, they still are a large producer of wine.

While wine was first produced in the United States and Canada in the mid-16th and early 17th centuries, wine production in North America was not established to any significant degree until much later. Spanish missionaries started a vineyard in California in 1769, with other immigrants eventually introducing varieties from France and Italy as well. By the late 19th century the wine industry in California was thriving, although there was little wine production elsewhere in the country. Even today, while wine is made throughout the United States, 90% of the country's wine is produced in California.

In Canada, the wine industry was not truly established until the late 20th century. Early attempts to grow wine-making grapes were largely unsuccessful, and a general prohibition on alcohol in the early 20th century prohibited the development of the industry, followed by restrictions on the general alcohol industry that were present until the 1970s. Eventually, grape varieties were established that could grow successfully in Canada's cooler climate, and the industry had expanded substantially by the 1990s. Today most wines in Canada are grown in Southern Ontario (particularly the Niagara region) and British Columbia, with the most successful Canadian wines being ice wines.

While wines produced in North America were long thought to be less palatable and of lower-quality than wines produced in Europe and even South America; today both

Canada and the United States produce wines that are recognized for their quality throughout the world.

Why has Wine Risen in Popularity Over the Years?

Over the years, wine has become more and more popular. A lot of families and friends have changed their social settings, even deciding against going out to bars in favor of gathering with a group at home for a few glasses of wine. Wine is a much more formal and sophisticated drink, which means you can enjoy it in a different environment, rather than a bar or club.

Although it is considered more sophisticated, it is often served at parties, business functions, and weddings. It is also used in cooking to add or enhance flavors. It is often looked at as a more health-conscious choice than beer or liquor. However, some of the main reasons that wine is chosen over other alcoholic alternatives are:

1. Lack of Choices

Some see wine as the only alternative. If you are health-conscious, there is no alternative better than wine if you want to enjoy an alcoholic beverage. Red wine can actually be a benefit to your overall health. Studies show that having one glass of red wine a day is a healthy additive to your diet.

If you look through history, during ancient times, there was no actual alternative to wine. Meaning there if there was no potable water to drink the only other option was wine.

Today, clearly we have options, but from a health perspective, we are limited in our choices. Wine is a much healthier choice than beer or liquor.

2. Progress and History

Many people just love wine and love to try the various types. People that are wine drinkers enjoy the development of new wines, the historical aspect of wine, and trying wines from different regions. Wine-drinking is much different than other alcohol drinking. You must learn how to drink wine to enjoy it fully.

3. Christianity

From a biblical sense, many wines are grown and produced specifically for the religious sacrament. Christianity requires the use of wine during their religious ceremonies.

For this reason, a large amount of wine is produced specifically for this purpose.

4. Opulence

Wine is also seen as a symbol of wealth and luxury. As we look back in time, wine was used as a symbol of the same thing. The upper and middle classes were the people that drank the wine. The drinking of wine signifies something more. Today it does the exact same thing, which makes it a popular choice among successful people.

Chapter 3

The Production Of Wine

<u>Wine Making Process</u>

You may think that the winemaking process is quite simple, and although in theory it is, there are some important steps that must be followed in the process. The process of making wine from grapes is called vinification, and it will vary based on region. Various regions will change the harvest times, type of oak barrel used for aging, type of grapes used, etc. However, every vinification process will include the following steps:

1. Choose Your Grapes

    One of the most important things in vinification is choosing the right grapes. In fact, it might be the most important step in the entire process, because the grapes that are used will determine the quality of the wine. The quality is determined by the growing season, the weather, soil, harvest time, pruning, etc. The combination of these factors is referred to as the grapes' *terroir*.

The type of grape that you choose will also, of course, affect the type of wine that you produce. Red or black grapes are used to produce red wine, with the grapes being fermented with their skins to get the dark color. White grapes are used to produce white wine, and the skins are removed as they are not needed to produce color. Red grapes can occasionally be used to produce white wine, which is achieved by extracting the juice without contact with the grapes' skins. Red grapes may be used to make rose wines by allowing the juice to stay in contact with the skin long enough to pick up some coloring.

Harvest times will vary based on location. The southern hemisphere will harvest from February to April and sometimes into May if it is too cool. The northern hemisphere will harvest from August into September.

2. Harvesting

Harvesting at the right time is very important for making good wine. Some regions still do this by hand while others use machines to pick the grapes. Technology has made it quite simple for machines to gather all of the grapes from the fields. However, most winemakers like to hand pick their grapes because the machines can actually be destructive to the grapes and vineyards.

Mechanical harvesting is done by large tractors which straddle the grapevine trellises and dislodge the grapes using rubber or plastic rods. The advantages of mechanical harvesters are that they allow the winemakers to harvest large areas of the vineyard during a short period of time, and they required a minimum amount of manpower to be invested in the harvesting process. However, the use of mechanical harvesters often results in the inclusion of non-grape materials in the gathered crops – these materials can include stems and leaves, but also moldy grapes, rocks, and even possibly birds' nests or small animals. Some winemakers will go through the grapevine before the mechanical harvesters are used and removed as much debris as possible by hand, but this then increases the time and use of manpower. Winemakers must balance the different factors to determine whether manual or hand harvesting is best for them. Mechanical harvesting is more common in areas where there are general labor shortages, such as New Zealand and Australia.

Manual harvesting is done by hand picking the grape clusters from the vines. For larger vineyards, bins as large as one or two tons may be used to transport the grapes to the winery. The advantage of manual harvesting is that it not only allows for the removal of debris, but if knowledgeable labor is used it also ensures that only properly ripe grapes are included, and unripe or rotted grapes are left out. The disadvantage, of course, is that can take much longer to harvest crops than mechanical harvesting.

The decision as to when to harvest the grapes is made by the winemaker. Factors that the winemaker will take into consideration include the levels of Titratable Acidity, sugar (the "Brix" of the grapes), and pH. The winemaker may also look at the grapes' ripeness, flavor, and tannin development (determined by the taste and color of the seeds). The overall health of the grapevine and even weather forecasts may also be taken into account.

Once you have all of your grapes in the winery, it is time to sort and cut out the rotten and under-ripe ones. You only want the best grapes for your wine. If you use unripe grapes, your wine will be spoiled from the start.

3. Destemming the Grapes

    Destemming is the process of removing the stems from the grapes. This can also be done manually or by machine. Again, as with picking grapes, it is better to do this manually so that the quality of the wine is not compromised. Depending on the region some winemakers like to leave a portion of the stem on to increase the wine tannin.

4. Crushing

    Crushing is an important step in the process because this is the process that extracts the juice from the skin of the grapes. Most people equate this part to people stomping on grapes, as you might have seen on television shows. Today, machines are used to extract the juice. In the crushing process, the grapes are gently squeezed to break the skins, so that one can access the fruit.

It is important that the skin is not torn too much during crushing because this will increase the amount of tannin, which is not good for white wine. The skin tearing will also cause the juice to oxidize, which is also undesirable. There are also times when grapes are only partially crushed so as to preserve the flavor.

The crushing and destemming processes are different depending on whether it is red or white wine being produced. For white wine production, the grapes are crushed, and the stems are usually placed into the press with the grapes. Having the stems included allows the juice to better move past the flattened skins, which gather at the edge of the grape press. When producing red wine, the stems are usually removed before fermentation as the stems generally have a high tannin content as do red grapes, so the inclusion of the stems would allow for too high of a tannin level.

5. Pressing the Grapes

Pressing grapes is the process of separating the skin from the juice. This is done by applying pressure to the grapes. Machines are used to help perform this process because it can be done much faster today than many years ago when it was done by h and. Again, you will want to be careful that you do not use too much pressure on the grapes. The more pressure, the more tannic the wine will turn out to be.

Pressing is not always required in winemaking; the free-run juice produced during the crushing process can be used and is usually of higher quality than the pressed juice. However, most wineries will also press the grapes because this allows for a greater production volume; pressed juice provides between 15% and 30% of a grape's total juice volume.

A grape press positions the skins (or whole grapes, depending on the process) between a movable surface and a rigid surface, and gradually moving the two surfaces toward each other. Modern presses have settings that monitor and determine the pressure of each stage in the pressing process, and the duration of each stage as well. The amount of tannin that is extracted increases as the pressure on the grapes increases, so modern presses have been developed to be very specific in exactly how much they press the grapes.

Before today's modern presses were developed, presses were made from wood and were operated manually. The presses were usually basket presses, which comprised a fixed plate topped by a cylinder of wooden slates and a moveable plate that could be forced down toward the fixed plate. The winemaker would place the grapes into the press and then lower the moveable plate downward until the juice came out through the wooden slats.

Some modern presses have incorporated the basket design because it is believed that this was a gentler process overall.

In red wine production, the juice is pressed after the primary fermentation process to separate the liquid from the skins, stems, seeds, etc. With white wine production, the liquid is separated from those materials before fermentation.

Another pressing technique is called pigeage, which is a French term for the traditional stomping of the grapes in large fermentation tanks. This technique, which combines the pressing and fermentation stages, is still used in the production of certain types of wine today, although foot stomping generally is no longer done. The grapes are put through a crusher, then poured into the fermentation tanks. As fermentation occurs, the grape skins rise to the surface, pushed by the carbon dioxide produced in the fermentation process. This layer of solids is referred to as the "cap." Because the cap is the source of tannins, if tannins are required (i.e. for white wines, usually), the cap will not be removed but will be mixed with the liquid ("punched") once a day.

6. Fermentation

After you have pressed your grapes, you can begin to ferment the juice. This is when the grape juice is converted into alcohol. The yeast interacts with the sugar in the grape juice, converting it into alcohol and carbon dioxide. The temperature and speed of fermentation are important.

There are two stages of fermentation. The first stage, called Primary Fermentation (Aerobic), lasts about three to thirty days depending on the wine. During this phase, the lid to the vessel is left off because air helps the yeast cell multiplication. About 70% of the entire fermentation process will take place during this stage. You may notice some foaming during this time. The longer the wine is in fermentation, the drier the wine will be, because more sugar will convert to alcohol. The shorter the amount of time the wine is in fermentation, the sweeter the wine. Every gram of sugar creates a half-gram of alcohol. This helps determine how long the wine needs to be in fermentation.

The final 30% of fermentation will take place in the second phase, called Secondary Fermentation (Anaerobic). This process will take about three to six months, and it will depend on the number of nutrients and sugar being converted. During this phase, you should cover the vessel. This is when the protein will be broken down, which creates clearer wine. This step should take place in an oak barrel or a stainless steel vessel with oak chips. For wineries with any substantial volume of production, the fermentation should take place in vessels that have a volume of several cubic meters. Whether stainless steel or oak is used depends on desired end taste. If only a minor oakiness is desired, the majority of the fermentation can take place in stainless steel vats with the wine to be placed in oak barrels only toward the end of the fermentation process. Oak chips can also be added to stainless steel barrels, although this technique is generally used only in cheaper wines.

The second phase of fermentation is when sparkling wine and Champagne get their bubbly characteristics.

The fermentation process differs between red wine and white wine production. After the primary fermentation of red grapes, the grape juice that has been extracted through the crushing process (called the "free-run juice") is separated and transferred into tanks, and the skins are pressed further to extract additional juice. The winemaker will then blend the pressed juice with the free-run juice in proportions that depend on each winemaker.

Another fermentation process is malolactic fermentation, which takes place when lactic acid bacteria convert malic acid to lactic acid. This is done intentionally by adding strains of the bacteria to maturing wine, although it can also happen accidentally if the lactic acid bacteria happen to be present.

Malolactic fermentation is used in wines that have high levels of malic acid, which causes a bitter taste. This process is used in the production of all red wines because they naturally have very high levels of malic acid. White wine production may also use malolactic fermentation; this technique is usually used for fuller-bodied white wines, which tend to have higher levels of malic acid.

7. Purifying and Refining

At this time, any solid portions of the grapes that are left over after fermentation are now removed by using a large filter. Some winemakers may choose to siphon off or add other substances that help facilitate solids sticking together and sinking to the bottom.

During this phase, winemakers may choose to combine other wines to create a preferred flavor, tannin level, or acidity. Additives can be added to enhance the wine flavor, smell, etc. Champagne is one wine that needs to be racked a certain way so that the lees (yeast sediments) will settle in the bottleneck. However, champagne can be filtered like any other wine, but the right racking creates a better taste.

8. Preserving

Most wines will have a label on the bottle indicating that they contain sulfates. For example, the United States requires it because sulfates can cause asthma attacks in about 3% of those that have severe asthma.

Two of the most commonly used preservatives are sulfur dioxide and potassium sorbate. Sulfur dioxide is particularly advantageous because it acts as both an anti-microbial agent and an anti-oxidant. In white wine production, it can be added either prior to fermentation or immediately after the alcoholic fermentation stage is completed. If sulfur dioxide is added after the alcoholic fermentation, it will stop malolactic fermentation (an advantage in white wine) and spoilage from bacteria.

The ideal level of sulfur dioxide should be 30 mg per liter of wine, and this level should be monitored and maintained until the bottling process.

In red wine production, sulfur dioxide can be added at higher levels initially, but then the level should be reduced to and maintained at 20 mg per liter. Sulfur dioxide is added either prior to fermentation or after malolactic fermentation. If done before fermentation, it will assist in stabilizing the color of the wine; if done after malolactic fermentation, it will help to prevent bacterial spoilage.

Potassium sorbate is more effective in controlling fungal growth, including yeast. This is of particular use in sweet wines. However, if sorbic acid happens to present during malolactic fermentation when the wine is bottled the sorbic acid can metabolize with the sorbate to produce geraniol, which causes a potent and unpleasant taste. To avoid the production of geraniol, the bottling process must be completely sterile, or sulfur dioxide must be added to prevent the bacteria from growing.

9. Premarket Aging

Wines are usually aged prior to sale. Generally, they are stored in oak barrels after purification for aging. Although some winemakers will use metal vats, concrete tanks, or glass contains to increase flavoring, the most common container is an oak barrel. Aging causes the wine to soften and slowly oxidize. Oak barrels also provide more flavoring. The aging process of better quality wines can actually continue after bottling.

While the wine is aging, periodical tests will be run on it to check the status of the aging process and ensure that the wine is aging properly. Tests that may be run include examining the pH, Titratable Acidity, sugar, sulfur, and alcohol levels. Depending on the test results, the winemaker can take appropriate action. If sulfur levels are too low, for example, sulfur dioxide can be added. Most winemakers will also perform "sensory tests" (i.e. looking at and tasting the wine), and may make changes to the wine based on those results.

10. Bottling

Finally, bottling can occur and during this phase, another round of sulfite is added to prevent any fermentation in the bottle. They are then sealed and corked for protection (or screw caps are used). The top of the wine bottle is usually heated to get a tight seal to reduce any chance of ruin.

Colors of Wine

Wine is known for its many color characteristics. The color of wine is determined by the grapes used during the vinification process and how long the grape skin is in contact with the juice. The process of transferring color agents from the skin of a grape to the juice is called maceration. The color of the wine changes depending on how long the grapes are pressed, aged, the vinification process and the techniques used in making the wine. The longer wine ages, the browner the wine becomes.

The main colors of wine include the following:

- White Wines:

    o Greyish Yellow – Pinot Grigio

- Greenish Yellow – Sauvignon Blanc

- Pale Yellow – Colombard, Gruner Veltliner

- Lemon Yellow – Riesling, Gewurztraminer

- Light Gold – Chenin Blanc

- Golden Yellow – Chardonnay, Viognier, Semillon

- Gold – Dessert Wines

- Brownish Yellow – Sherry, Mature White Burgundy

- Amber – Vin Santo, Toklaji

- Brown – Malaga, Marsala

- Rosé wines:

  - Onion Skin – Rosé Champagne

  - Salmon – Rosé Syrah

  - Raspberry – Rosé Grenache, White Zinfandel

- Red Wine:

  - Copper – Aged Grenache

  - Brick Red – Mature Pinot Noir, Aged Bordeaux

- o Garnet – Cabernet Sauvignon, Merlot, Nebbiolo

- o Ruby – Young Pinot Noir, Tempranillo

- o Cherry – Sangiovese, Zinfandel

- o Purple – Barbera, Amarone

- o Blackish Red – Shiraz, Vintage Port

Types of Wine

Most wines are classified by the grapes used to make the wine and where the grapes were grown. Wines that are based solely on the grape variety used are known as varietals and wines based on the region of growth are named by the region. There are various types of wines and styles, but, there are two main categories, known as red and white wines. You can then categorize wines by the taste of wine as well. The sweetness of wine can vary based on the grapes that were used to make the wine. There are three classifications of wine by taste: dry wines; medium wines; and sweet wines.

Generally speaking, wines can be broken down into the following six types: red wine; white wine; rosé wine;

sparkling wine; sweet wine/dessert wine; and fortified wine.

Red Wines

Red wines are made with red grape varieties (there are hundreds of varieties) that will result in various shades of red wine. The varieties and taste are determined by the winemaking process but are typically light to dark and dry to sweet. The variation is very wide. The four most popular red wines are:

- Cabernet Sauvignon
- Merlot
- Pinot Noir
- Zinfandel

White Wines

White wines are normally colorless, or at least yellow or gold in color. White wines are made from white grape varieties, although some are made from red grapes, but the pressing time is limited, and the skin of the grapes is not allowed to touch the grape juice. This reduces any redness in the color of the wine. White wines can range from sweet to dry. The four most popular white wines are:

- Chardonnay
- Riesling
- Pinot Gris/Grigio
- Gewurztraminer

Rosé wines

Rosé wines are often called "blush wines" because they are not true red wines. They have a red tint to them making them different than white wines, but they are certainly not a red wine even though they are made from the same grapes. The vinification process is different than that of red wine. The most popular rosé wine is a Zinfandel.

Sparkling Wines

Champagne is the most popular sparkling wine in the world and is used at many celebrations and is one of the most common wines used for that purpose. They have more carbon dioxide in them than other wines, giving them a fizzing effect. The most popular sparkling wines are:

- Rosé Champagne
- Prosecco
- Sparkling Red Wine

Sweet Wines/Dessert Wines

Sweet wines are made from the residual sugar left behind from the production of other wines. This is why they have such a sweet taste. The amount of sweetness varies by wine, and they can be off-dry to incredibly sweet. The most popular sweet wines/dessert wines include:

- White Wines:
  - Botrytis (Nobel Rot)
  - Ice Wine (Eiswein)
  - Late Harvest Wine
- Red Wines:
  - Late Harvest Wines
  - Fortified Wines

Fortified Wines

Fortified wines are those that have grape spirit added to them (such as brandy). They come in both dry and sweet. The most popular fortified wines include:

- Port Wine

- Madeira
- Sherry

Table Wines

Table wines generally have a lower alcohol content than other wines. They are usually sipped on during dinner and are served with food. Table wines are not as expensive as other wines, making them widely popular all over the world. In the United States, table wines are not fortified wines or sparkling wines and are seen as good quality. Some other countries, like Europe, see table wines as lower quality. Some of the most popular table wines are:

- Cabernet Sauvignon
- Merlot
- Chardonnay
- Adams Apple
- Muscat
- Port
- Pinot Noir
- Kaskaskia Concord
- Double Decker Red

Common Wines

Some wines are more common than others. These wines are typically bought and served, produced and blended for purchase more than others. The wines described below will give you an idea of the range of flavors available.

Cabernet Franc

Cabernet Franc is an essential part of the Bordeaux blend family of red wines that are produced out of the United States. Cabernet Franc is not usually consumed by itself because of its tannic nature in the United States. However, in Europe, it is known for its strong violet and blueberry taste. Its tannic characteristic is what makes it so distinctive. Surprisingly, it often smells like fresh coffee. It is made as a varietal in portions of France but is not labeled as such. In other parts of France, it is blended with Merlot giving it a spicier, pungent taste. Again, Cabernet Franc is a popular wine that is well known and used as a blend.

Cabernet Sauvignon

Cabernet Sauvignon is the most common and well-known grape in Napa Valley, California and it is one of the most used grapes and wines in Bordeaux, France. Cabernet

Sauvignon is grown all over the world but has only achieved great success in particular locations. This is because it ripens late and is weedy. In France, Cabernet Sauvignon is blended to reduce its intense tannins. However, in the United States, it is known for its dark black jam color that tastes like black cherries. It is a very thick wine with a strong scent and flavor. This grape helped define wineries in California and Washington in the United States.

Gamay

Gamay is the grape of Beaujolais, a small portion of France. It is a young wine that should be consumed very close to its production. It is a fruity wine that tastes of strawberry, raspberry, and cherries. If made using the carbonic maceration technique, it will have a slight banana smell to it, making it even more unusual. Beaujolais Nouveau is the most famous Gamay wine and is released each year just after harvest.

Grenache/Garnacha

Grenache and Garnacha are red wines of Spain and Australia. Each are also blended for several other popular wines in France, such as Châteauneuf du Pape, Gigondas, and Côtes du Rhône. Grenache and Garnacha wine have very high alcohol content and low acidity because of the wine grape. They are fruity wines that have a slight spice to them. Grenache and Garnacha wines are known as softer versions of Syrah.

Malbec

Malbec is not a very popular wine in most regions, but is very prominent in Argentina because they tend to make spicier tart wines. Malbec tastes like sour cherries. This wine ages extremely well in oak barrels, where it gains more of its characteristics. Some Malbecs are made in the United States on the West Coast.

Merlot

Merlot is one of the most popular red wines and gained popularity during the 1990s. It is extremely popular in France and in the United States. This grape ripens very well and creates a powerful wine that will age for a very long time. Merlot generally tastes like watermelon or strawberries. Some say it does not have a lot of character, but it remains fairly popular.

Mourvedre/Mataro

Extremely popular in France and Spain, Mourvedre and Mataro taste like spicy cherries. They are medium-bodied wines that are generally used in blends. They are not popular wines, but are still produced in the United States on the West Coast and in Australia. The wines blend well with Shiraz and Grenache.

Nebbiolo

Nebbiolo is the most popular grape in Italy and is one of the most popular red wines in the world. It is a hard variety of grape to grow anywhere else. For some reason, when other regions around the world have tried to produce it, it comes out light, thick, and bland. Italy produces it to perfection with a plum, cherry pie taste.

Pinot Noir

Pinot Noir is the most demanded wine, but one of the most difficult to make. It is originally produced in France, but even in France if winemakers are not careful, their wine will be ruined before it even has time to age. The grape is very unpredictable, which makes it difficult to produce. It is the principal blend in Champagne and other sparkling wines. It can also ripen longer to produce other wines that are of thicker nature. Pinot Noir is best as a varietal and is made in the United States, France, and New Zealand. It can age for decades as well, which is why it is also a popular wine choice.

Sangiovese

Sangiovese is the wine grape of Tuscany, Italy and the main wine grape in Chianti and Brunello di Montalcino. It is a lighter color wine and is known for it is distinct cherry pie taste with a touch of tobacco flavoring. Some winemakers have trouble getting that specific flavor, leaving it quite bland. Sangiovese is often blended with Cabernet Sauvignon as well, balancing the two wines out and making a pleasant mixture.

Syrah/Shiraz

Syrah is made in the United States. It is generally a spicy, peppery tasting wine with blackberry, boysenberry, and plum flavorings. Syrah is known as Shiraz in Australia. Australia has made several styles of Shiraz, including light wines to dark wines, with more or less fruit flavoring. It is generally a deep red sparkling wine and often is a fortified

"Port" wine. The wine will always have a tart or pepper spice to it.

Zinfandel

Zinfandel is one of California's most prominent grapes. It is grown in the United States, Australia, Italy, and many other places in the world. However, the wine made in California is the model that all others follow. Zinfandels can vary depending on production region. Some are drier with a hint of Asian spice, while others are fruitier. The thickness of the wine changes as well. In Napa the wine is thicker, using sweet black cherry flavors. The alcohol content in Zinfandel wines is usually 15% or more.

Chardonnay

Probably the most popular white wine, Chardonnay is grown and produced all over the world including France, the United States, and Australia. It typically smells like fresh green apples and tastes of similar citrus flavor. During fermentation, it also picks up a vanilla scent from the barrels. Chardonnay is one of the most popular wines in the world.

Chenin Blanc

A wine common to France that is good for blending. It can be produced both dry and in a sparkling wine or dessert wine manner. It usually takes on apple, lemon, and pear taste for a fruitier flavor and smells of flowers. It is rather acidic, making it more of a dessert drink.

Gewurztraminer

The Gewurztraminer grape is extremely popular in France because of its floral smell and spicy taste. This wine can be extremely dry or as sweet as you like it. In the cooler climates, such as the United States and Italy, the wine tends to be more fruity and sweet than it does in France. This is a very popular wine that is often paired with foods.

Marsanne

Marsanne is a fairly new labeled wine in parts of the world, such as the United States. Typically, it is blended with others such as Roussanne, Viognier, and Grenache Blanc. However, Marsanne is a full-bodied white wine with low acidity that tastes like peaches and pears, which has made it popular for blending in France and the United States.

Australia has planted this grape for many years, making it one of the oldest in Australia.

Muscat

Muscat has many varieties, but they all smell of oranges. If Muscat is fermented dry, the wine will have a fruitier taste and smell to it. This is often done on purpose to create the perfect wine. It is a great sparkling wine or dessert wine, for example, Moscato d'Asti and Beaumes de Venise made out of Italy.

Pinot Blanc

The Pinot Blanc is a lighter version of Chardonnay with a green apple, citrus taste. This wine is made in Italy and parts of the western United States (California and Oregon). In the United States, the Pinot Blanc takes on a little bit of spicy taste as well.

Pinot Gris/Grigio

Pinot Grigio is a complimentary dinner wine because it offers a fresh citrus and melon taste that is great for your palate. The best version of this wine comes from Tre Venezie and Germany. The Pinot Gris is a pear-flavored wine with a bit more sweetness and fruity taste than its sister, the Pinot Grigio.

Riesling

Riesling is one of the most popular wines available because it can be dry or very sweet with green apple, citrus, apricot and peach flavors. This wine can age for long periods of time because it just gets sweeter with time and it does not ruin. Riesling wine production is the best in Austria, the United States and Europe.

Roussanne

Roussanne is a popular French grape and the wine is made throughout southern France. It is quite popular on the western seaboard of the United States as well. It is a full-bodied lime and citrus tasting wine. It is a great blending wine and is very good with Marsanne.

Sauvignon/Fume Blanc

Sauvignon Blanc is grown all over the world and can create a wide array of flavors depending on its ripeness. Some flavors include grass, herb, citrus, pineapple, and peach. Some of this has to do with the soil and harvest techniques used in production. In New Zealand, Sauvignon Blanc is the most popular wine. It is often produced in California, but most notably with a peachy, tropical taste. Sauvignon Blanc is blended with Semillon to create Sauternes, some of the most famous sweet wines in the world.

Semillon

Semillon is often a dry, white wine known for its grassy aroma and herbal taste. If it is not fully matured, it will have a fig or melon taste to it. However, it can be harvested later and used as a dessert wine. It is typically blended with Sauvignon Blanc. Semillon is produced in the United States and Australia.

Viognier

Viognier has a unique aroma and tastes of flowers, citrus, apricots, and peaches. It is important that these grapes are fully ripened before fermentation because if they are not, the taste can turn quite bitter. This wine is made in the United States and Australia. Viognier is often blended with Syrah to create another red wine as well.

Gruner Veltliner

Almost entirely grown in Austria, Gruner Veltliner is best when grown in its native location. However, it is also grown in small amounts in the Czech Republic, United States, and Slovakia. Typically, this wine tastes of green grape and apple flavoring with some peach and citrus additions. The better versions of Gruner Veltliner are those wines that are produced and then aged for a long time in oak casks. The flavoring will change a bit, adding a white pepper or spicy characteristic that works well with the fruit taste.

Serving Wine Temperature

The serving temperature of wine greatly affects the taste of the wine. Most people enjoy their wine served at room temperature and this is generally the right temperature for the best taste because it brings out the smell, flavor, and structure of the wine.

However, some wines need to be served at a different temperature depending on the type and its characteristics. It is important that you understand what temperature to serve your wine at, so that you do not ruin it. Understand that wines served warm are difficult to chill, but those wines that should be served chilled easily warm. Therefore, you need to be careful when you serve your wines so that they taste their best. Wines have specific tastes that can easily be ruined if not served at the appropriate temperature.

It is recommended that you follow these rules for serving wines:

- Red wine should be served between 55°F - 63°F
- White wine should be served between 43°F - 50°F
- Rosé wines and full bodied white wines should be served between 46°F - 55°F
- Ice and champagne wines should be served between 43° - 46°F

NOTE: Temperatures can fluctuate a degree or two.

Red Wine Serving Temperature

The type of red wine you are drinking will determine the serving temperature. Most assume that it should be served at room temperature, but this is not always the case. Typically speaking, you should serve your red wine at a little bit colder temperature than room temperature because it will warm. Wine will always get warmer more easily than you can cool it. The warmer you serve red wine the more you ruin the freshness of it, and you will lose the aroma and flavor.

Never serve red wine above 65°F because it will change the flavor and taste of the wine. It is best to put the bottle of wine in the refrigerator or an ice bucket and then warm your glass before pouring the wine. This way you keep your wine cool and you can warm it as needed. You can always cool your wine before you serve it for dinner or lunch, just remember how much time you need. If you drink wine on a regular basis, I recommend purchasing a wine rack with the correct storage compartment so that you can keep your wine at the correct temperature so that you maintain the characteristics of your wine.

More specific guidelines serving your wine:

- Light wines such as Beaujolais should be served at 55°F
- Medium bodied red wines such as Chinate, Pinot Noir and Zinfandel, should be served at 60°F
- Full-bodied red wines such as Bordeaux, Cabernet, Merlot and Shiraz, should be served at 63-65°F

For a better understanding of when to serve various red wines use the following guidelines:

- Red Sparkling Wines — served at 45°F
- Sweeter Red Wines — served at 45°F
- Lighter Bodied Red Wines — served at 60°F
- Fuller Bodied Red Wines — served at 65°F

<u>White Wine Serving Temperature</u>

White wine is the opposite of red wine in that you never want to serve it too cold. Although you can drink it at a temperature colder than red wine, you do not want it too cold. In fact, it is best to serve it too warm than too cold. If you do serve it too cold you will not get the full effect of its flavor and taste. White wines should never be served at less than 45°F because they will lose their fresh, sweet taste and smell.

Although it is okay to store your white wine in your refrigerator (unless your refrigerator is extremely low), it is best if you let it warm for 30 to 60 minutes prior to drinking it. Drinking it directly from your refrigerator is not advisable. Look into getting a wine storage compartment of some kind, which is talked about later in this chapter.

Understand that most white wines such as Sauvignon Blanc, Chenin Blanc, and Vinho Verde decrease in flavor if they are over chilled. Some wines will even ruin if they are over chilled, so be very careful when storing your wine. Do not to store them in areas less than 45°F.

Of course, champagne and sparkling wine are different and can be served cold. Taking care of wine prior to drinking it will make the experience much more enjoyable when you pop the cork.

Sparkling Wine Serving Temperature

Sparkling wines can be served a little colder than white wines. You can enjoy sparkling wine directly from your refrigerator at about 40°F. These wines will not lose their flavor if they are cooled; however, you will actually see a little bit of improvement if you let them warm just slightly. I recommend letting the wine sit for 15 to 20 minutes so that you get the intended bubbly effect!

Remember there are various types of sparkling wines. Some of them are slightly better at various temperatures.

White sweet and aromatic sparkling wines, such as Asti Spumante, should be served at 46°F. These wines can be served at low temperatures because they are aromatic. They will not change in flavor.

Red sweet sparkling wines, such as Brachetto d'Acqui, should be served between 50°F and 53°F. Again, the wine can be served at a lower temperature because it is aromatic.

Tannic sparkling wines should be served at temperatures higher than 57°F. The cooler temperature will ruin the taste.

Dry sparkling wines, such as Prosecco di Valdobbiadene e Conegliano, should be served between 46°F and 50°F to preserve their flavoring.

Any time a wine is made using a "Classic Method" and "Methode Champenoise," the wine should be served between 46°F and 50°F.

Any special vintage wines should be served around 53°F because that will increase the aroma that arises during the aging process. Nonvintage wines can be served between 40°F and 44°F.

Dessert & Fortified Wine Serving Temperature

Dessert and fortified wine serving temperatures are little more difficult to choose. The real issue is that there are a large variety of wines and the temperature greatly affects the taste and aroma. Therefore, depending on those two characteristics, you need to select the right temperature.

In general, if the wines are light and fruity you can serve them at a cooler temperature and if they are more complex and heavier, it is suggested that you serve them at a warmer temperature.

- Light-bodied sweet dessert wines – served at 43°F - 50°F
- Dry fortified wines — served at 48°F - 52°F
- Medium-bodied fortified wines — served at 50°F - 54°F
- Full-bodied dessert wines – served at 46°F to 54°F
- Sweet fortified wines — served at 61°F - 65°F

Wine Storage Today

The quality of your wine is greatly affected by the storage location. Over time, the color of wine will change, the smell will become stronger, and the flavor will change. The temperature of the location and the bottle it is in will affect whether or not the wine can reach its full potential. Wine storage should be about 55°F with not much fluctuation and a cork should be placed at the top of the bottle to prevent airflow. Most wine cellars are dark for a reason; the light will affect the characteristics of your wine as well, so it is best to keep the wine in a dark location.

Wines are produced for consumption in about a year, which is much different than in the past. Wine is ready to drink as bought while they are young. However, for a red wine to reach its full maturity you can let it sit for four years. White wines are good in about two to three years from their date of vintage.

Wine storing options are unlimited today. Some people have wine cellars where wine bottles are placed on racks free of vibration, light, and temperature fluctuation. The door can be closed for protection and is only entered when wine is retrieved. Some people even have closet wine cellars now, where you can dig a large hole in the basement if a larger wine cellar is not an option. Now they even make special wine refrigerators that maintain a constant temperature. The lighting is reduced and the humidity inside is monitored. These are great for consistent wine drinkers.

There are options available and it is worth looking into if you want to fully appreciate all of the characteristics of wine and the full effects wine has to offer.

The Evolution of Wine Storage

The origin of wine storage is fun to examine and essential to understand why storage is useful and needed today. Today we focus on temperature, humidity and vibration, but in ancient history, they focused more on storing for the sake of storing regardless of the technology. They also wanted to be able to transport it easily.

One of the oldest known wine glasses is called the wineskin. They were made out of animal skin or bladders from animals to store the wine. Although they did not hold up over time, they were used quite often and for a long period of time. They were portable and convenient for many years.

For the storage of wine after production in large quantities, a large clay vase container called a Kvevri was created. This was found by archeologists in the country of Georgia as some of the oldest wine pottery in the world. These were used for grape crushing, fermentation, and storage. They were capped with large wooden stoppers and then buried underground for aging purposes. This would help regulate the temperature, protect it from the elements and it was found that this enhanced the aroma, flavor, and characteristics of the wine.

Amphorae containers were created during the ancient Greek and Roman Empire eras. They were tall, slender clay vessels that were used to store standardized sizes of wine. They were specifically created for the international trade business to ship overseas. The large clay containers even had handles so that they could be moved and carried. The thing that made these unusual was that they were not set on the ground, but hung in the air during shipment to make the shipment more reliable. They were less likely to break and when it was time to store them once they got to their destination, the curved cylinder shape made them easier to bury for further aging. These were used for decades and have been found all over the world.

Today we use oak barrels for storage and this started during the Roman expansion. The Celts invented the wooden barrel. This was a third-century novelty that became the norm for wine storage and aging. Oak was used because of its availability at the time, but today it is used because of its characteristics. So it was by accident that the aging process that oak played on wine actually happened.

After we use oak barrels for the aging process, we now store wine in glass bottles for sale. This started in about 100 B.C. by the Romans, when they would take a molten lump of glass, attach it to a long hollow pole and blow into it to form glass bottles. This practice did not officially become an invention until 3,000 B.C. Glass was still not used much at that time because the act of traveling with it was so difficult. These bottles were more of a decorative item than anything else. By the 17th century, coal-burning furnaces brought glass bottling to a new focus. Glass bottles could be made thicker and more resilient than before, making them more of a viable option. The use of glass bottles and aging changed what bottles looked like for wine. The long sleek look that we use today was developed because of the aging process and the ability to store wine on its side to avoid spoiling it.

Corks are the finishing touch on any wine bottle. In the earlier day's wooden stops were used, but prior to that, they used grass, wood, wet clay, or other substances to cork wine. The creation of the cork changed wine storage because it could keep the airflow out of the glass bottle and keep the humidity down.

In essence, oak barrels, glass blowing, and the creation of the cork really paved the way for a new foundation of winemaking and storage.

Chapter 4

What Makes A Good Wine

Great wine really has to do with the grape selection, the winemaking technique used, its long-term vision, and the art associated with making it. As discussed in previous chapters you need good, high-quality wine grapes to make an excellent wine. You also have to use production techniques that adequately ferment and age the wine. Also, as with any business, great winemakers have strategic plans. Those that can think into the future generally develop their brand with exceptional wine. The art of winemaking means that it is a craft. The more you learn about wine, the more you realize there is a science behind it. Just like preparing food or music, it takes careful preparation, ingredients, and ideas to create fine wines.

The primary element of wine is the wine grape. Two things make wine grapes quality wine grapes: terroir and vintage. Terroir really encompasses the climate surrounding the grape, the soil, and other natural aspects which affect its growth. The second aspect is its vintage, which involves human interaction much more than the terroir. The vintage includes pruning, soil treatments, harvest time, irrigation, etc.

More About Terroir

The terroir component of wine really encompasses three main characteristics: soil, climate and flora. The flora includes the plants, fungi, grasses, trees, and flowers in the area. This even includes the yeast and bacteria on the grapes.

Climate can be broken down into three different climate levels: macroclimate; mesoclimate; and microclimate. Vineyard wine grapes grow better at different temperatures. Therefore, macroclimates include the average temperature a region is during growing season. Macroclimates tell us which grapes grow better during which seasons and in which regions. Mesoclimates are a breakdown of the climate within a Macroclimate (region).

Macroclimates can have a variation in temperatures based on their region. The conditions and variations that change inside Macroclimates affect grapes, which is why there are Mesoclimates. Things that affect Mesoclimates include vineyards that are located in valleys, are close to water, on slopes, and the direction they face. Microclimates directly affect the vines themselves.

The reason soil affects wine grapes so greatly is because the vines need to be fertile during growing season. There are four main soil compositions that are used in vineyards.

- Clay — soil that typically produces rich and structured vines
- Sand — soil that typically produces higher aromatic wines with a light color
- Silt — soil that typically produces a more vigorous vine with herb flavoring, however, it produces vines similar to clay soil
- Loam — a soil that is not typically used, but is often found in valleys and is sometimes mixed with clay or sand soil

Most of the ancient red wines such as Napa Valley, Tuscany, Burgundy, Pomerol, and Coonawarra were all grown in clay soils, whereas the more aromatic wines, such as Riesling and Beaujolais, were grown in sandy and rocky conditions.

The thing to remember is that the more complex your soil is, the more complex your wine will be. However, there is some debate about how fertile the soil should be and how deep it should be as well.

More About Vintage and Harvest

The vintage of a wine starts when you begin picking the wine grapes and will include all processes and preparation of making the wine. This is also called viticulture, the act of wine growing. Winemakers have to take timing into consideration. Grapes need to be picked before it gets too hot in warmer climates because they can over ripen quickly. This will cause them to lose their freshness and fruity flavor. In cooler regions, winemakers need to be careful of heavy rains. Grapes need to be picked at the right time.

Harvest also has to do with the phenolic ripeness, which must be taken into consideration as the grapes are picked. This has to do with the tannins in the grape. The grapes which have less ripe seeds and skin will taste bitter, which means that they have low tannins. Wines with high tannins are those which have full ripeness in the seeds and thicker skin. For example, Cabernet Sauvignon and Nebbiolo are high in tannin and Pinot Noir is low in tannin.

The viticulture of a vineyard must be sustainable to be profitable. This means that it is environmentally responsible, meets social equity standards, and is economically viable. A winery that does this is making a commitment to reduce the wastefulness and use natural organic ingredients in its winemaking process. A lot of vineyards are permaculture so that they are self-sufficient and rely only on the ecological and environmental resources to sustain them. There are certificates that explain the type of sustainability that a vineyard is.

During the fermentation process, winemakers want to reintegrate the juice from the wine grapes with the leftover seeds and the grape skins. To do this, two different methods can be used: punch down or pump over. Both are a process used to stir the cap (the skins, seeds, stems, etc. from the grape) back in with the juice. However, different grape varietals need a different level of extraction to fully develop the flavors. So, the punch down or pump over method needs to be used for different wines. For example, Bordeaux varieties of Cabernet Sauvignon, Merlot, Malbec, and Petit Verdot should use the pump over method while Pinot Noir, Syrah, and GSM blends are better with the punch down method.

Next, the fermentation temperature plays a vital role in the winemaking process. The yeast is what converts the sugar to alcohol. As the alcohol heats up, the temperature will increase, which will cause the smell of the wine grapes to burn off. The cooler the temperature the more you will preserve the fruit and flower aromas. The warmer the temperature, the less fruit and flower aroma remain and earthier smells are prominent. With this said, for example, red wines with a more floral smell are fermented at lower temperatures. Also, note that the more stems left on the grapes will also naturally decrease the temperature during fermentation.

The selection of an aging container is highly important to the final product. There are typically three main containers that winemakers use: stainless steel tanks; concrete vessels; and oak barrels. A stainless steel tank is used to preserve flavors and is mostly used for white wines because the floral and herb smells are so important. Concrete vessels are used for those wines that have fruitier characteristics, such as red wines that have a bit more texture after the aging process. Last, oak barrels, which are probably the most popular, are used to increase the oxygen in the wine and increase the flavors because most of them are caramelized. This creates new flavors such as smoke, tobacco, coke, and vanilla. Choosing the tank for aging is ultimately up to the winemaker, but it is one of the most important steps in the process because it can make or break the taste and smell of the wine. The biggest decision is how much oxidation a winemaker wants and whether or not they want to preserve its natural flavors. This is really where a winemaker can add their own unique touch to their wine.

Blending may need to be done to the final product, before bottling, in order to achieve the winemaker's desired taste. Wines made from different types of grapes, or even batches of the same grapes made under different conditions, can be combined to correct inadequacies in the individual wines. Blending can range from making minor additions to adjust tannin or acid levels to complete blends of different varieties or vintages for a unique taste.

Next, a winemaker must make the decision as to whether the wine will be fined and filtered. A good wine will have a fining agent added to it so that the particles will bind together and fall to the bottom of the wine. Those particles will stick to the bottom of the tank, vessel, or barrel creating a clear wine. Fining also helps to reduce astringency or tannin levels, if necessary.

The fining agents are usually a protein of some sort, possibly casein from milk or egg whites. The type of fining agent (or agents) that are used depend on the winemaker, and will vary between varieties of wine and even possibly batches of wine. Gelatin is a traditional fining agent that is still used today and is popular because it is also very good at reducing tannin levels. For the most part, no gelatin will be left in the wine once the fining process is complete because it produces a sediment that can then be removed by filtration before the wine is bottled. Other animal products that can be used as a fining agent include bull's blood, bone char, sturgeon bladder, and skim milk powder.

There are also non-animal-based filtering agents, such as diatomaceous earth or cellulose pads.

The wine can then be poured through a large filter with microscopic holes to catch any particles. Most white wines, rosé wines, and sparkling wines are fined and filtered to perfection. However, not all red wines go through this process. A lot of winemakers go through this process because it truly stabilizes the wine. However, others believe doing so takes the texture out of the wine. Either way, the winemaker makes the call and more often than not this process is performed to reduce the cloudiness from the wine. Wines with a clear finish are much more enjoyable.

Last, but not least the wine is bottled. The biggest decision with bottling is the cap. Do you cork or cap it? Most high-quality wines will have a cork while the lower quality wines will have a screw cap. However, both work and many winemakers use both methods.

Rutherford Winn

Chapter 5

Top Wine Regions In The World

Every year more and more countries begin producing wine, but ten countries are routinely producing at least 80% of the world's wine. The top three countries for several years in a row have been France, Italy, and Spain; producing just under half of all of the world's wine. The three of them make enough wine to fill over 5,000 Olympic-sized swimming pools.

The top-producing regions do change, depending on climate, advances in winemaking techniques, and other factors. It is interesting to keep an eye on up-and-coming wine regions, such as the Gobi desert. However, the top production areas have remained relatively stable for the last few decades. It is useful to know these regions if you are really into wine because it may guide you on wine-related travel.

France and Italy continue to compete for the top spot, but they are both reducing wine production each year. For example, France has reduced production by about 11% since 2007 and Italy have reduced its production by 7% since 2007. Both countries have been removing vineyards over the last few years.

Spain has the largest vineyard acreage in the world but produces much less wine than both France and Italy. The United States hosts one of the largest wine producers, Gallo. Gallo is located in Modesto, California. California produces 90% of all of the wine produced in the United States.

Argentina is continuing to grow its wine production at the rate of 8% per year but heavily relies on its exportation business as does Australia. Australia has typically exported to the United States, but with a weakened dollar, Australia has since exported to Hong Kong and Asia as well. Germany is well known for its aromatic wine. They also focus on their exportation business.

South Africa is the largest producer of Brandy in the world and produces the popular Chenin wine as well. Germany is best known for its aromatic white wines, which are exported primarily to the United States and the United Kingdom. Chile produces a red wine variety called Carmenere, which is also referred to as the lost varietal of Bordeaux, but it is not as marketable as traditional varieties.

Dessert wines are highly popular which is where Portugal comes in. They are well-known producers of Port wine. Port wine is a very alcoholic wine made of several blended varieties.

It is good to know where the most popular wines come from because you understand more about their value and quality. These countries have focused on the most integral parts of producing wine down to the smallest details, which is why they are the top producing wine countries in the world.

Knowing the varieties of wine that these regions produce, and particularly that they export, will help you to determine which regions produce the best of those varieties. For example, Spain produces the most

Tempranillo wine of anywhere in the world, and it is a major export. You could take this to mean that Spain produces the best Tempranillo that there is because its production volume and export rates would not be so high if other regions were producing a better product.

When choosing which wines to buy, do not focus just on the fact that these regions produce the most wine; pay attention to the varieties in which each region specializes, so that you can make sure that you are getting the best possible wines.

China has become a large consumer of wine but has recently become a large exporter of wine as well. The popularity of wine in China partially has to do with its economic incline. Wine has historically been seen as a symbol of upper class and sophistication.

Below is a list of the major wine grapes used in the world by country.

Major Wine Grapes in the World

Country	Grapes
Italy	Sangiovese, Trebbiano

Spain	Tempranillo, Airen
United States	Cabernet Sauvignon, Chardonnay
Argentina	Malbec, Chardonnay
Australia	Shiraz, Chardonnay
Germany	Riesling, Muller-Thurgau
South Africa	Chenin Blanc, Colombard
Chile	Cabernet, Chardonnay
Portugal	Port Grapes, Alvarinho

<u>2015 Top Wine Producing Countries</u>

France and Italy have been the top producing wine countries for the last several years. However, there are some changes happening in other producing countries. Europe seems to be declining in production, though. A reason could be the decline in consumption and that for years there was an overproduction of wine. Europe accounted for 73% of the wine production in the early 2000s, but now Europe is only contributing to about 60% of the world's wine production. The United States, Argentina, and South Africa are all on the rise. China is also a large producer of wine and continues to stay at the top of the list.

Based on research, wine is becoming more of a commodity and less of a consumed product in the countries where it is produced, and this is changing rapidly. In the early 2000s about 25% of the wine that was produced was exported, but now that is up to roughly 40%. There is a changing landscape for wine, and international trade means wine is being shipped all over the world.

Basically, all this means is that there is diversity in the wine world. Production is not going down; we are just seeing a transformation in where wines are being made and who is consuming the wine.

2015 International Organization of Vine and Wine (OIV) World of Wine Producers

Italy	49,500
France	47,500
Spain	37,200
United States	22,140

Argentina	13,358
Chile	12,870
Australia	11,900
South Africa	11,200
China	11,000
Germany	8,900

*volume in thousands of hectoliters

2015 Top Wine Exporting Countries

The wine exporting market is heavily dominated by the top three countries: Spain; Italy; and France. Between the three of them, they export almost half of the entire wine export volume. Sales and volume are different animals, though. Spain does not seem to do as well sales-wise because their revenues actually fell just a bit from the prior year. All three of these countries have numerous wineries with a competitive edge for exporting their wine. The biggest challenge is branding and understanding international trade business.

2015 International Organization of Vine and Wine (OIV) World of Wine Exports

Spain	24,000
Italy	20,000
France	14,000
Chile	8,800
Australia	7,400
South Africa	4,200
United States	4,200
Germany	3,600
Portugal	2,800
Argentina	2,700

*volume in thousands of hectoliters

Chapter 6

The Cost Of Wine

The cost of wine varies greatly based on its quality, production costs, distribution costs, retailer costs, etc. There are different categories of wine. The category the wine is in will determine its expensiveness be. Much of the determination is based on its cost of production (because production has everything to do with its quality) and the cost of its distribution.

There are nine categories of wine: extreme value, value, popular premium, premium, super premium, ultra-premium, luxury, super luxury, and icon. The prices range from less than $4 a bottle to over $200 a bottle (based on the value of a dollar in the United States).

Extreme Value Wine

Some examples of extreme value wine include those from the Gallo Vineyard, Sutter Home, Crane Lake, Tisdale, Rex Goliath, and boxed wine brands. All of these will cost you $4 or less per bottle. Most of these wineries have huge commercial production factories with distribution centers that are quite reasonable. These wines are often blended with several nonvintages, grapes, and regions. Most of these are produced out of California and are a mix of wines. There is nothing special about these wines, and they are wines for a younger generation.

Value Wine

In the value wine spectrum there is a lower side and a higher side. On the lower side, there are brands such as Black Box Merlot, Barefoot, Lindemans, and Yellowtail that will cost you in the $4-$8 range. Those brands tend to have more sugar. The higher value brands will cost you $9-$10 and are a bit better quality because they come from the finer wineries in the United States, France, and Italy. These wines are specifically for your everyday drinking made from single vintages from larger regions.

Popular Premium Wine

Premium wines will cost you between $10 and $15. This category is the biggest market for most buyers. Most of the wines in this category are decent varietal wines from worldwide production wineries. Some wines are inflated just because their bottles and the labels are visually appealing. They are commercially overrated. There are a lot of people that do not know much about wine and buy based on the look of the bottle and label. A lot of wines in this category go above and beyond in presentation so that they are bought. These are a lot of the so-called "white label" wines. If you want a good popular premium wine, it is suggested that you pick wine that focuses on a region. For example, North Coast or California. The specificity means that the wine is a little bit more high quality. A few examples of good wines in this category include De Loach Pinot Noir, Beaujolais Louis Jadot, and Chateau Ste Michelle Cabernet Sauvignon.

Premium Wine

Premium wines are the start of the higher end wines and cost between $15 and $20 per bottle. These wines will have some high ratings because of the vintage, and most of them will be from focused regions in the world. These will have more flavor and aroma than your lower category wines. The red wines will be oak barrel aged from wineries that take extra care in selecting and harvesting their wine grapes. Sauvignon Blanc, Grenache, and Shiraz are some wines that are available in this category.

Super Premium Wine

Super premium wines are those wines that are handmade from medium to large production wineries around the world and cost between $20 and $30 each. They take extra care in every step of the production process to ensure the wines are top notch and prepared to perfection. The quality is excellent, and you will definitely find wines with exceptional tastes, aromas, and that are spot-on for their regions of craftsmanship. Some of the more notable super premium wines are Donnhoff Reisling Dry Slate, Chateau Thivin Cote de Brouilly, and Hentley Farm Shiraz.

Ultra-Premium Wine

Ultra-premium wines are those that you find stored in someone's wine cellar or wine storage rack for about $30 to $50 per bottle. These are of excellent quality, with unique tastes and are opened on special occasions. These are the kinds that you can let age for a while before opening, and they do not need to be opened within a year of purchase. Some examples of ultra-premium wines include Groth Cabernet Sauvignon, Chateau Margaux Brane Cantenac, and Cristom Pinot Noir.

Luxury Wine

Luxury wine is pretty expensive at $50 to $100 per bottle. However, this amount of money will buy some of the best wine in the world from some of the top producers. You can also get some wines that are special or unique to vineyards and aging requirements or those that are in high demand for certain varieties. These are some of the most pristine wines in the world, and you will be in company with some of the wealthiest people in the world as they tend to buy this type of wine. Some popular wines in the luxury wine category are Keenan Cabernet Sauvignon, Rudi Pichler Riesling, and Billecart-Salmon Blanc De Blancs. These are some of the tastiest wines you will ever have the pleasure of drinking.

Super Luxury Wine

Super luxury wines are produced from some of the top producers in the world that are worth $100 to $200 each. These wines are made in some of the most famous and revered wine regions in the world. These wines are severed at the best restaurants around the world as well. Some of the wines in this category include Vosne-Romanee IER CRU Aux Brulees Domaine Bruno Clavelier, Aubert Chardonnay, and Rinaldi Barolo.

Icon Wine

At $200+ per bottle, this wine is the pinnacle of all wines. This is the best of the best you will ever drink. If you ever want to try the best wines of your life, try one of the following: Petrus Pomerol; Clarendon Hills Astralis; or La Grande Dame Champagne.

Is Expensive Wine Worth the Money?

Although most wine enthusiasts will agree that a more expensive bottle of wine will taste better than a lesser expensive bottle of wine, those that are not wine enthusiasts do not necessarily believe that a more expensive bottle of wine is worth the money. Research shows that the main reason for this is the residual sugar that is put in the cheaper wine. Residual sugar is used in cheaper wines to improve the taste, so for those that do not drink a lot of wine, this wine may taste just fine.

The problem with this approach is that most wine drinkers associate the "richness" of the wine with its sweetness. Therefore, because cheaper wines use residual sugar to achieve the sweetness, it can inaccurately reflect that the cheaper wine's quality is as good as the more expensive wine's quality.

With that said, are the most expensive wines worth your money? First, you need to understand why some wine is more expensive than others. Let's take for example a $10 bottle of wine and a $35 bottle of wine. The cheaper bottle of wine is produced in a large production environment using American oak or no oak at all for fermentation. There may be a little aging time, and most likely none at all. The harvest process is entirely machine handled, and all of this is done in a general location such as California using quality grade grapes. The bottles used are cheap with a cork and capsule that only cost about $1. The wine aging process only contributes to roughly $3 of the costs and the markup value on the wine is about $4. With that said, you know this is extremely cheap wine. As for the $35 bottle of wine, it is produced in a small vineyard, fermented in a French oak barrel. The wine is given time to properly age and is hand harvested in Napa Valley using premium grade wine grapes. The bottles used are a little bit higher end, and the cork and capsule are more expensive to keep the air and humidity at a minimum, costing about $5. The wine aging process contributes to roughly $11 of the entire cost, and the markup is roughly $17.50.

Clearly, the value of the more expensive wine is much better than the cheap version. Understand that the grape quality is much better, the production of the wine takes longer, and the winemaking techniques used are more focused on quality as well. Although large quantity production of wine is good at times, those producers have to produce at a profitable margin. This is why the quality of the wine is compromised. Smaller scale production that is more focused on the harvest process must mark their wine at higher prices, or they will have losses.

Think about the type of wine you want to drink and that will help you determine if you want the cheap version or the more expensive version. The more expensive version is always going to be better quality, but until you can adequately tell the difference, it may not matter. If you are taking it to a party, a wedding, as a gift, or something similar, I would definitely recommend buying a more expensive wine.

Rutherford Winn

Chapter 7

How To Read A Wine Label

Wine labels provide consumers important information about the wine. The label tells you what kind of wine it is and its origin. In fact, the label is the only thing you can rely on to determine which wine you want to purchase. The label provides you with vital information, which will help you with your selection. The more you learn about wineries and their wine the more the label will help you.

There is certain information that must be put on the label required by law, and this information will vary by country. For example, the United States requires that the label includes the brand name, type of wine, bottling information, alcohol content, and net content. The Alcohol and Tobacco Tax and Trade Bureau of the US Treasury

Department (TTB) regulates wine labels in the United States. In Europe, the European Union wine laws require that the quality of wine be printed on the label as well.

There are actually three different wine labeling types: varietal-based; terroir-based; and sheer fantasy. The varietal-based labeling technique is fairly easy to understand, and it is used specifically for varietal wines. This wine labeling technique was pioneered in California, and most New World producers use it. However, as mentioned in other chapters of this book, in order for wine to be a varietal it must be made with no less than 75% of one wine grape in the blend (this may differ by country). That wine then takes the dominant grapes' name. The label of a varietal-based wine is the most common and includes the brand name, vintage, estate where it was bottled, appellation of origin, varietal designations, name and address, alcohol content, net contents, health warning statement, and declaration of sulfites.

The terroir-based labeling technique is extremely informative except that it does not provide you with the varietal information. Most European wines use the terroir-based labeling technique. A terroir-based label will have the chateau classification, a drawing, name of chateau or vineyard, appellation, appellation controller certification, chateau logo, bottling information, the volume of the bottle, owner of the vineyard, export country of origin, and lot identification number. It is a more complex labeling system that can be hard to understand by many.

Fantasy labels will provide you with the producer when it was established, their name, where the grapes came from, the color of the wine, and the alcohol content. This label will vary widely, but this is an example of what could be provided on a fantasy label. The label will not tell you about the grapes or the blend of grapes used.

In the United States, a typical wine label will include the following information or similar to the below (varietal-based labeling):

- Brand Name
- Type of Wine
- Country of Origin
- Vintage
- Fanciful Name
- Special Designations
- Vineyard Designations

- Producer
- Bottler
- Estate Bottled
- Alcohol Content
- Net Content
- Declaration of Sulfites
- Government Warning

Labels will come in all shapes and sizes, but if you learn what type of wine you like, you will be able to read the labels and determine what wine you should buy. Below is a breakdown of what is on American wine bottle labels.

Brand Name

This is the name of the wine that is used to market and identify the wine.

Type of Wine (also known as Variety or Appellation)

The type of wine will be the varietal name such as Cabernet Sauvignon, Zinfandel, or Chardonnay, or a generic name given to it by the winemaker. This refers to the kind (or kinds) of grape used to make the wine. Many blends do not indicate the grapes used, or if they do, they will not show the percentage of each type of grape. Just remember, as stated above, if a winemaker uses the varietal, 75% of the content has to be from that designated grape. If no varietal is given, you can look to see if there is an official appellation indicated. There are fifteen countries that have officially regulated appellations, and those appellations have rules about which varietals can be used. If one of those appellations is used, you will be able to determine which varietal (or varietals) were used in the production of the wine.

Country of Origin (Appellation of Origin) This is the place where the dominant grapes were grown. This could be a country, state, or region. States and countries can be put on the labels for those wines that are varietals. For those wines that received at least 85% of their content from an American viticultural area and the wine was finished in the location of the AVA, a special designation of American viticultural area (AVA) can be used. For example, this could be something similar to Napa Valley. California requires that all of the grapes used in wine that you want to label with its origin as California, or any geographical subdivision of the state, must come from within California.

Generally speaking, wine that is sourced from a larger (i.e. vaguer) region will be a value wine; the more specifically that the source of the grapes is identified, the higher the quality of the wine. Some wine labels go so far as to specify a specific vineyard, which usually indicates a particularly refined wine and is therefore accompanied by higher prices.

Vintage

The vintage date is the harvest date of the wine grapes. For typical wines, a blend can include 15% of another vintage. Those wines that are labeled American viticultural area (AVA) are held to a stricter guideline. Some wines will indicate "NV" (Non-Vintage), which means that they are a blend of multi-vintages. This means that the wine is a lower value because the ease of production is higher: rather than being restricted to the options available to the winemaker during the production of that specific batch; the winemaker had the option to blend wines from different vintages to overcome any deficiencies.

Fanciful Name

The fanciful name is often used by the winemaker to differentiate the wine from other brands.

Special Designations

Special designations are not required, but can be used to indicate the sweetness or color of the wine. This is a place to indicate if it is a reserve wine or a special selection wine. The "reserve'" indication does not actually mean much because there are no official rules as to what can and cannot be called a reserve wine. Small producers often use this term to indicate their highest-quality wines, blended from their best quality production wines and aged in their best barrels. However, other wine producers may also use the term to convince purchasers that their wine is of high quality. Always take a "reserve" indication with a grain of salt.

The "Old Vine" (or "Vielles Vins") is another indication which should be taken with a grain of salt because again there are no rules that dictate how old the vine has to be in order to get that designation. Generally speaking, "Old Vine" means that grapes from older vines were used, which produces more concentrated flavors. However, wines with this designation can be produced from vines ranging from 15 to 115 years, and some may be a blend of old vine grapes and young vine grapes. As with the "reserve" indication, tread carefully when selecting a wine based on this designation.

Vineyard Designations

Some wineries decide to name the vineyard where they grow their wine grapes or an independent owner who owns the vineyard. Either way, some winemakers choose to add the vineyard name to the label to designate where the grapes were grown. To do this, 95% of the grapes must be grown in that vineyard.

Producer and Bottler

The wine label will always have the bottler and its location, but there are various descriptions that are used to indicate more information. Any of these are acceptable:

- "Produced and bottled by" – This will certify that the bottler fermented the wine at least 75% at a specific location.

- "Cellared and bottled by" – This will certify that the bottler subjected the wine to particular cellar treatment in accordance with their processes at a specific location.
- "Made and bottled by" – This will certify that the bottler fermented at least 75% of the wine at a specific location.
- "Bottled by" – This will certify that the winery bottled the wine at a specific location.

The producer's name will either be obvious, or it will be written in a small text at the top or bottom of the label. Most French wines, for example, use a smaller text. Some American wine labels will include only the name of the wine, and no information about its producer; this usually means that these are branded wines produced by larger wine companies. You can easily look up the producer of these wines.

Estate Bottled

This term is used to indicate that the winery grew all of the grapes on its land, crushed, fermented, aged and finished the production process of the wine, including bottling. On French wines, the label may read "Mis en Bouteille au Château," "Mis en Bouteille au domaine," or "Mis en Bouteille a la Propriété." On Spanish wines, a common indication is "Embotellat a la Proprietat," Italian wines will likely read "Imbottagliato all'origine," and German wines will indicate "Erzeugerabfullung."

When you see that wine has been bottled on an estate, this usually indicates a higher value wine, at least compared to wines which are not estate bottled.

Alcohol Content (also known as Alcohol by Volume, or ABV)

A statement indicating the percent of alcohol content must be included, such as 12% ALC./VOL. When wine has an alcohol content of 7% to 14% the winemaker may choose to put "Table Wine" or "Light Wine" instead of an actual alcohol percentage. While it may seem to be a relatively straight-forward aspect of the wine, the ABV can actually tell you a lot about the wine. For example, in Europe often only the highest quality wines are allowed to have an ABV of 13.5% or higher. In America, on the other hand, the ABV is often quite high, with some dry wines having an ABV as high as 17%, so it is less of an indication of quality than for the European wines. The ABV can also be an indication of how rich or full-bodied the wine may taste, as wines with higher ABVs are often made from riper grapes, which tends to provide a stronger fruit flavor. This is a generalization, of course, and there are exceptions to these rules.

Net Content

Net content is the fluid volume in metric measurements included in the bottle. However, wine can only be bottled in specific measurements: 50 ml, 100 ml, 187 ml, 375 ml, 500 ml, 750 ml, 1 L, 1.5 L or 3 L.

Declaration of Sulfites

If wine contains a level of 10 or more parts per million of sulfur dioxide, an indicator must be placed on the label that says "Contains Sulfites." In the United States, this is not a particularly helpful designation because the label must be put on all imported or domestic wines, and most grapes happen to naturally contain sulfites. Generally speaking, if someone has not had a problem with dried apricots or mangos, which have levels of 1,000 to 4,000 parts per million sulfites, then even high-sulfite wines (with levels of only 300 to 400 parts per million sulfites) will not be a problem.

Government Warning

Based on government regulation, all wine bottles must have a health warning statement that says the following:

"**GOVERNMENT WARNING:** (1) ACCORDING TO THE SURGEON GENERAL, WOMEN SHOULD NOT DRINK ALCOHOLIC BEVERAGES DURING PREGNANCY BECAUSE OF THE RISK OF BIRTH DEFECTS. (2) CONSUMPTION OF ALCOHOLIC BEVERAGES IMPAIRS YOUR ABILITY TO DRIVE A CAR OR OPERATE MACHINERY and MAY CAUSE HEALTH PROBLEMS."

National or Regional Classifications

For "Old World" (i.e. European) wines, the labels can be particularly difficult to interpret. This is because many of the wine-producing countries in Europe have various classifications for their wines, which are fairly strictly regulated and indicate the quality of the wine. In Italy, for example, there are the DOCG, DOC, IGT, and Vino da Tavola classifications, and in France, they have AOC, Vin delimité de qualité superieure, Vin de Pays, and Vin de table. France has further sub-classifications, to make things even more complicated. Portugal, Spain, and other countries also have similar classifications.

France's classification of AOC (or Appellation d'Origine Controlée) indicates the highest quality wines produced in the country. Currently, just over 50% of all French wines fall within this classification. To be considered an AOC wine, the grapes must have been grown in specific areas and only certain varieties of grapes can have been used for this classification. Other factors include production method, minimum alcohol level, vine age, harvesting, and storage techniques.

The next highest quality classification is VDQS, or Vin Delimité de Qualité Superieure. This is very rare today, with less than 1% of French wines falling within this category. The classification is similar to AOC, with fewer restrictions on the varieties of grapes used, terroir, and wine production techniques.

Vin de Pays, or VDP, is a classification that indicates that the wine was produced in a major, specific wine-growing region, and the label must state the producer's name and that the wine was made in France. There are few other restrictions on this classification.

Finally, Vins de Table (now called VSIG, or Vins Sans Indication Geographique) are the lowest quality wines produced in France. The producer's name will be provided on the label, along with the information that the wine is from France, but not the location or region within France where the grapes were grown, or the wine was made. There are no restrictions on the types of wines that fall under this classification.

The Italian wine classifications are very similar to the French ones. DOCG, or Denominazione di Origine Controllata e Garantita), is the highest quality classification. There are stringent rules applied to wines that wish to fall under this classification, and usually, the priciest wines are DOCG. DOCG rules restrict the allowable yield of grapes, require more extended aging periods, and perhaps most importantly, require that the wines pass a tasting and analysis by someone licensed by the government before the wine can be bottled with such high distinction. In addition to these requirements, DOCG wines must be sealed and have a numbered government stamp on the cork, to ensure that the wine is not altered in any way after the tasting and analysis have been carried out.

DOC, or Denominazione di Origine Controllata, is the next highest quality classification. This classification requires that the wine is produced in a well-defined and specific region of Italy. The problem with this classification is there are actually hundreds of different DOC appellations, so the DOC classification itself does not give you a lot of information about the wine. All it can really tell you is the general level of quality of the wine.

The next classification is IGT, or Indicazione Geografica Tipica, which means that the wine is a typical wine from that specific region. IGT wines are generally fairly simple and do not age particularly well; they are great wines for an everyday meal, decently priced but nothing too special.

The lowest quality classification for Italian wines is VdT, which stands for Vino da Tavola. This classification means "table wines," and so is the same level of classification as the French VSIG classification. The only requirement for VdT wines is that they are made in Italy, so there really is no guarantee as to the quality of the wine. These wines are generally quite inexpensive.

Other Information

One useful piece of information that will be found on many labels is suggested food pairings. While this may not be particularly helpful if you do not have a specific meal in mind with which you will be drinking the wine, it is very useful if you are picking out wine for a planned meal. This information will usually be found on the "back label" of the bottle.

Chapter 8

Wine Tasting

Wine tasting is a sensory craft that is learned and the more you drink wine the better your tasting abilities will become. It is often an acquired taste as well. Wine tasting has been around just as long as its production. In fact, history states that a formal methodology of wine tasting started in the 14th century. In recent years, however, modern professional have a highly evolved and specific terminology that they use to describe the perceived aromas, flavors, and general characteristics of the wine. Wine tasting events are held all over the world. Typically these are open events where people can come and try a variety of wines for fun. However, professional wine tasting events are typically served blind. This means that the judges cannot see the label, bottle shape, or color of the wine because those details can lead to an early prejudice just by knowing more about the wine. Professional wine tasters can detect what type of wine they are being served just by seeing these details. Plus, blind tasting reduces any price bias, color bias, geographic origin bias, etc. Professional wine tasting events score the wine on three different aspects: the appearance of the wine; nose or smell; and palate or taste. Then they are given an overall score. Depending on the event, the weight of each factor is different.

There are several factors that affect the taste of wine, such as the temperature of the wine itself, the ambient temperature, the type of wine glass you use, foods and your psychological and physical state.

When you taste wine, you are really evaluating five different characteristics: color; aroma; taste; body; and aftertaste. These considerations will allow you to determine the character and complexity of the wine, the wine's potential (suitability for drinking versus aging), and any possible faults of the wine.

After you have determined the characteristics of the wine that you are tasting, for a thorough tasting you should also compare it to recognized standards for that type of wine and wines within its price range. For example, you could consider whether the wine-making techniques used, such as malolactic or barrel fermentation, are standard or whether the wine was produced using unique techniques.

While you can taste wines on their own, it is usually recommended to compare wine with several other wines at the same time, to get a more objective assessment of the wine. This is what is known as a tasting "flight." The wines that you will taste together can be chosen based on their vintage, which is known as horizontal tasting, or the winery at which they were produced, which is known as vertical tasting. If you wish for a truly blind tasting, you will of course not want to be informed as to how the wines have been chosen until after you have completed the tasting.

If you are conducting a blind tasting, the level of "blindness" can vary. Usually, this means that at the very least, you will not see the label or the bottle. However, the color of the wine can also be hidden by serving the wine in a black wine glass, so that you are blinded to even that factor. It is up to you whether you want to be able to assess the color of the wine, which is one of the factors that are often considered in a tasting, or whether you want to be completely blind to the wine that you are tasting.

Blind tasting is useful because, as mentioned above, it prevents price bias, color bias (if going fully blind), and geographic origin bias. Studies have clearly shown that each of these biases exists if tasters are given the information ahead of time. For example, in 2001 the University of Bordeaux conducted a study of 54 undergraduate students, asking them to test one red wine and one white wine. The participants consistently commented on the difference between the two wines, even going so far as to discuss the "jammy" flavor the red wine. In fact, the wine in both glasses was white wine, with the "red wine" having been colored by a flavorless dye.

Geographic origin has also clearly been established through scientific studies. At Texas A&M University, a study was done over 6 years wherein various people were asked to taste wines that were labeled as being from Texas, California, and France. The "French" wine was consistently rated as the highest quality wine. In fact, all of the wines were the same wine, which had been produced in Texas.

Color

The color of the wine you taste should give you an indication of its maturity and age. A pale white wine is fairly young in age while golden white wines are older and have aged longer. Dark red wines are young in the aging process while older red wines are more amber in color. Pay special attention to this as you try different wines. You will get an idea of what age your wines are as you try a multitude of types.

Aroma

Wine will always have a distinct aroma, but different wines have specific smells. Those that have distinct smells that give away its flavor are the ones that are top quality. You take long deep inhales to enjoy the quality of the wine. Do not just sniff your wine, but take the time to enjoy the smell thoroughly. If you do it right, you should be able to taste it during your inhale.

Taste

Tasting wine is a process, which we will get into in more detail later in this chapter, but you must understand how to taste wine properly. The alcohol, sugar, tannin, acids, and flavors all balance together to create a beautiful design of character. Blends are strategically placed together to even out the attributes.

Body

The body of a wine describes the thickness, texture and consistency. These are all determined by the alcohol content, sugar content and tannin. There are different bodies of wine: light (under 12.5% alcohol content); medium bodied (12.5% to 13.5% alcohol content); and full bodied (over 13.5% alcohol content). Each wine will vary, and as you try different ones, you will learn what light versus full-bodied means.

Aftertaste

The aftertaste of wine leaves a lasting impression and this attribute truly reveals the quality of wine. If the wine has a good aftertaste that lasts for a long period of time, it is generally a better wine. If the aftertaste is bad or does not last very long, the quality is not nearly as good. This is a secret that many wine drinkers do not know. Pay special attention to this one.

While the above are the more specific factors that you will be assessing when wine tasting, there are overall characteristics to which you should also pay attention, and which will be assessed by looking at all of the above factors in combination. The varietal character, for example, refers to the extent to which wine puts forward its inherent grape aromas. Integration should be present in the wine, which means that none of the wine's components (tannin, acid, alcohol, etc.) are out of balance with the others. If the wine is well-balanced and has good integration, this is known as 'harmonious fusion'.

The wine's expressiveness is another important quality. This refers to the wine's flavors and aromas being clearly projected and well-defined. Complexity is another consideration; a more complex wine will have multiple flavors, and how well they blend and complement each other must be assessed. Finally, the connectedness of the wine may also be considered, although this is usually left to true connoisseurs and professionals as it is a difficult quality to ascertain: it refers to the connection between the wine and its terroir and it is hard for any but the most refined tasters to assess this.

Other characteristics that are usually left to the true connoisseurs include the assessment of faults like oxidation, cork taint, or preservatives, the results of which may be noted by the average taster but it may be difficult to identify the specific cause of that result.

Tasting Conditions

It is important that each time you taste a new wine, your palate is clean and fresh from any other tasting conditions you have been eating or drinking. This will have a dramatic impact on how good or bad a wine tastes. Also, the temperature of the wine when you serve it is highly important. Refer to Chapter 3 for more information on wine serving temperatures. Also, if there are any strong smells or scents nearby, it is suggested that you remove those so that you can adequately smell the wine you will be tasting since the aroma is such a large part of the evaluation process.

The shape of the wine glass can have a subtle but noticeable effect on your perception of the wine, especially when it comes to the wine's bouquet. The ideal glass shape for tasting wine is wider at the bottom, and narrowing at the top – i.e. an egg or tulip shape.

Evaluating Wine

The tasting process follows what is referred to as the "five S steps:" see; swirl; sniff; sip; and savor.

Evaluating by Sight

After you pour a glass of wine or are given a glass of wine, you need to examine the wine. It should only be filled about one-thirds of the way full. The first thing you will do is look down into your glass at the wine, then hold it up to the light, and finally tilt the wine glass so that the wine can roll onto the edge of the glass. This allows the wine to move freely giving you complete freedom to see its full color. If you are tasting a white wine, the color is best judged by putting it against a white background, in a well-lit room.

By looking down into your glass you can see the depth of the wine color along with its density and saturation. As you try different wines, you will be able to determine quickly what type of wine it is by its color.

By looking through the side of your wine glass and holding it up to the light, you will be able to see how the clarity of the wine. If the wine is not clear, it may have some chemicals in it, had some problems during fermentation, or is an unfiltered wine. It is always a better indicator of quality if the wine is clear.

When you tilt your glass and allow the wine to slowly thin out on the side of the glass, you will be able to determine the age and weight of the wine. Of course, it takes time to learn this, but if it is pale in color and is waterier looking the wine will most likely lack flavor. As far as color is concerned, if it is a brown color for a white wine and more orange or rusty for a red wine, then it is probably an older wine (or it has been oxidized). The more your try wines, the more you will learn about color. Over time, you will be able to tell if you are trying a newer or older wine.

Evaluating by Swirl

The swirl is one of the most important parts of trying wine. As you swirl your wine look to see if your glass has any "tears" that run down the side when you stop. If so, this means that the wine has a higher alcohol content and glycerin content. This also means that the wine will be a little bit bolder, riper, and more filling than others.

The swirl is also what helps aerate the aroma of the wine. You will be able to smell the flavors better when you raise the glass to your nose because the aromas will rest just inside the glass.

Evaluating by Smell

Now you are ready to smell your wine, but to get the full benefit, give your glass another swirl. If you are tasting a sparkling wine, make sure that you do not swirl it to the point where bubbles are released. Gently glide your nose over your glass in circular motions to get the full fragrance of the wine. Aroma in wine is actually called "stereoisomers," meaning they are mirror-images to other smells from our everyday lives. Take a few short sniffs and then hold it in before you exhale. There are a few key things you should look for while smelling the aroma from your wine glass.

The first thing you want to do is look for any spoilage, musty, or bad smells because this will indicate something is wrong with the wine. A couple of common smells that you may run across are SO_2, vinegar and Brettanomyces. Sulfur Dioxide (SO_2) will smell like burnt matches. If the wine has been bottled with a lot of sulfites, this will give the wine a burnt smell. If the wine has a large amount of acidity to it, you may smell vinegar. Last, Brettanomyces are added to red wines to give an earthy, leathery taste. However, sometimes too much is added during production causing it to overcompensate. You will no longer smell any of the fruit, but it will be a strong leather scent that is undesirable.

It is important that you learn how to identify the flaws in wine so that you can learn how to identify the positives. The more you learn about the flaws, the more you will learn about what you do and do not like.

Once you have established that there are no flaws in the wine you are evaluating, try to look for the fruit smells. Obviously, wine is made from grapes, but as discussed earlier in this book, there are a wide variety of smells that wines portray from bananas to cherry pie.

Wines also have floral aromas, so try to pinpoint what herbs and grassy scents are present as well. Those with floral aromas tend to fall into different categories such as herbal and grassy, earthy, mineral and rock, leather, etc.

Many wines also leave aromas from their aging process from time spent in oak barrels. Some of these scents include chocolate, vanilla, espresso, nuts, smoke, etc. These scents can still be picked out years later, depending on the time spent in the barrel, the type of oak used, the age of the barrel and the way the winemaker mixed and matched the wines.

Wines also establish secondary aromas. For example, some white wines that are young in age and sparkling wines will have a slight beer smell to them. Dessert wines occasionally have a honey smell and Chardonnays even have a popcorn or caramel smell. The older wine gets, the less fruity the aroma. A more mature wine is harder to identify because it loses part of its aroma over time.

With all of this said, it is important that you learn more about the different scents that each wine portrays. Take the time to smell as many as you can so that you learn and can begin to associate a scent with a particular wine.

Take your time to pause and really take in the 'nose' (bouquet, or aroma) of the wine, as this is a major determining factor in the perceived flavor.

Evaluating by Sip and Savor

Finally, now that you have fully appreciated the smell of the wine, it is time to take your first sip. Remember to sip your wine, do not take large gulps and do not swallow it right away. Wine is a sipping drink that should be savored. Take a small sip and circulate it around your mouth. Do NOT simply swallow it. You want to enjoy the taste and take in all of the flavors. The reason you do not swallow it is because the flavors may change. You will want to assess not just the taste of the wine, but its "mouthfeel" – the texture, weight, flavor, and structure of the wine. Hold the wine in your mouth for a few seconds so that your taste buds are saturated, then purse your lips and breath in through the small opening created. This will move oxygen over the wine, which will, in turn, release more esters. This allows the fullest profile to be available to your palate so that you can fully assess the wine.

Just as you saw before during your sniff test, you will taste a wide range of flavors from fruit too floral too earthy. The tastes will follow right in line with how they smell. Not only will you identify the actual flavors of the wine, but you also need to determine the following characteristics: is the wine balanced, harmonious, complex and completed?

As humans, we can detect sweet, sour, salty or bitterness in a wine because of our basic taste buds. A well-balanced wine will be both sweet and sour because of the residual sugar and acidity. A wine should rarely have a salty component to it and a wine should never be described as bitter. You may get an astringency taste from the tannins, but it should not be bitter.

A dry wine will give you a mixed bag of flavors in both taste and smell. They will have a much stronger taste than you realize just by smelling it. Sweet wines will have a subtler taste to them.

The thing to remember when tasting your wine is that it must have a balance between the flavors and it is important that the wine is not too much of one component. If the wine is too bitter, too alcoholic, too sour, or too sugary, the wine will not taste good. If this is the case, it is a good indication that whatever technique was used to make the wine was not done correctly, the wine is still young and has not aged properly, or it is too old and the wine has lost its luster.

If a wine does meet all of these requirements and all of the flavors seem to be well integrated, then the wine is harmonious. A good wine easily blends its flavors together, but you can still identify each flavor flawlessly.

A complex wine is one that changes flavors in your mouth and even after you swallow. A good wine taster is able to detect the initial flavors such as the ripe fruit and vanilla flavors. As you sip the wine and swish it in your mouth, you can detect additional flavors and those after you swallow. As a wine taster, you need to learn to wait to take your next sip until you have fully enjoyed the aftertaste of each sip. A complex wine will have flavors during each step of this wine tasting process and the flavors will linger.

Finally, a complete wine is one that meets each one of the before-mentioned components. A wine that is balanced, harmonious and complex. These wines are the best on the market because they are the best tasting and most satisfying wines you will ever try. They smell good, taste good, are clear, have a nice texture and the aftertaste is spot on.

While it may go against instinct, the proper way to conduct a wine tasting is to expectorate (i.e. spit out) the wine after you have tasted it. This is based intoxication can affect your judgment and ability to assess the wines that you are tasting, so expectorating the wine will reduce the intoxication effect. There will still be some intoxication, of course, because the wine is absorbed through the skin in your mouth. When attending a tasting, it is polite to ask where you should expectorate before you start the tasting. Usually, a spittoon will be provided, although not always. Sometimes you will simply be spitting onto the ground, but make sure to ask before you do that!

After you have completed your tasting, you should prepare your tasting note: this is your written notes that set out the taste identification, aroma, structure, acidity, texture, and balance of the wines that you have tasted. Taking down and keeping these notes will allow you to return to them when you are making a decision as to which wines to purchase, as it will be a reminder of which you enjoyed most. Some online wine communities even allow members to post their tasting notes online and to look at the tasting notes of others, for even greater knowledge of different wines. Some of the notes will of course only apply to the specific batch that you tasted at the time of your tasting, but they can still be generally helpful.

Scoring Wine

Through the tasting process, you will be able to give the different wines a score which will help you to compare them to other wines. The scoring system for wine tasting is relatively set, with four aspects to be evaluated: appearance, nose (bouquet), taste, overall. Different scoring systems will give greater percentages of importance to different aspects – e.g. 15% to appearance, 35% to the nose, and 50% to palate. In Europe, wines are usually scored out of 20, which is the total marks from each category, while in the United States the score is usually out of 100. Different critics may have their own preferred system. When looking at a wine's score as determined by someone else, you should consider that some wine ratings will have come from one specific critic, while others may be a combination of the scores from various critics.

Improving Your Tasting Skills

If you are interested in improving your wine tasting skills, there are a few different things that you can do. You can travel to different wineries and wine regions, and visit wine producers. The wine producers will usually be happy to offer tastings of their wines, sometimes at a cost and sometimes not depending on the winery. You can also attend a wine school, which will offer wine tasting classes, or your local college or university may offer wine tasting classes. There are also courses for training professional sommeliers and winemakers, if you are really serious about wine tasting.

I hope that you use the evaluation tips mentioned in this chapter to help you learn more about the art of wine tasting so that you are more efficient in the future. Take the time to experiment at home. Learn what you do and do not like. Take the time to focus on the characteristics of wine and you will learn to really enjoy wine tasting as a hobby. It is also helpful if you take the time to learn more about the wine flavors before tasting the wines so that when you do taste a wine you will appreciate it.

Rutherford Winn

Chapter 9

Wine Pairing with Food

Wine pairing is an art and you must understand how to balance the flavors of the food with the wine perfectly for it to work. Once you have mastered your understanding of wine and the different flavors, then you can start pairing it with food to make it even more enjoyable. Wine has been a staple at the dinner table for many years and in many cultures, however, most people do not know how to pair. In fact, most people do not even think about the type of wine they will be serving as they are cooking dinner. The art of pairing food and wine is relatively new, although it has long been a tradition to serve wine at the dinner table. The main concept is to present pairings that interact well together, which makes the experience much more enjoyable.

Remember that your wine flavors come from the sugar, acid, tannin, alcohol, and acid in the wine. Food is similar to wine in that the flavor components of food come from fat, acid, salt, and sugar. Your goal is to pair food and wine so that they complement each other in richness and texture. One of the most basic rules to remember is that it is better to progress through lunch or dinner with a light to heavy mixture. This means that you will start with serving white wines and end with red wines. It just so happens that chocolate desserts are perfect with sweet red wines!

There are six main elements of food and wine pairing based on the characteristics of food and how they balance with wine. The six elements are fat, acid, salt, sweet, bitter, and texture. In order to pair wine and food properly, you will need to learn more about these six elements.

Fat Element

High levels of fat are found in most of our foods, more specifically in foods such as meat and dairy products. Wine, naturally, does not contain fat, so fatty foods need to be balanced with a wine that is a little higher in acidity, tannin or alcohol than others. For example, a steak is served with Cabernet because the protein and fat merges perfectly with the wine's tannins. That works well with the wine's fruit and berry flavors which also compliments the smoky meat flavor from the steak.

Acid Element

Acid provides you with a kick of freshness and it does the same thing with food. If you add lemon to a fresh piece of fish, it adds an element of freshness. The lemon gives it more of a tangy taste. When selecting a wine to go with a food like this you need to make sure that you select a wine that is of the same value of acid or less so that the wine does not taste bland. For an acidic dish, it is suggested that you choose a wine such as Sauvignon Blanc or Semillon.

Salt Element

Salty dishes are hard to combine with wine because it eliminates the fruity taste from wines and makes highly alcoholic wines taste bitter. However, salty foods and sweet wines make quite a treat. One of the more popular salty and sweet combinations is blue cheese and Sauternes. Sparkling wines work great with salty and fried foods because of the carbonation and acids. This actually emulates what a beer does. Sparkling wine adds texture and flavor as well. The reason these work together is that acidic wines clean the salt from your mouth and balance out the flavors from the food and wine.

Sweetness Element

When you are serving desserts, make sure that the wine you serve is sweeter than the dessert itself. White wines, such as Chardonnay, make great dessert wines. Red wines and chocolate are pretty popular as well, such as Zinfandel. Just make sure that the chocolate is dark chocolate, not sweet. The problem you run into with sweet desserts is the degree of sweetness.

Bitterness Element

When wines display a bitter taste it is usually because the grapes were unripe, or some of the seeds may have been left in during fermentation. You need to be careful that you do not serve a bitter wine with a bitter food dish because this will just intensify the taste. There is no combination to make it better, just be careful not to make it worse.

Texture Element

As for texture, you will need to make sure you pair light with light and heavy with heavy. Therefore, you will serve a light wine with a light food and a heavy wine with a heavy food. You can always be adventurous and try to contrast the two, but you do not want one to overpower the other. The rule of thumb is to keep light with light and heavy with heavy.

Basic Food Pairings

Below is a listing of some of the most basic wine and food pairings. These are items that you can serve as snacks or for dessert. Use this as a guide for creating some pairings of your own. Have fun with it and feel free to mix and match as you like between the wine and food listings for each wine type.

Light Dry White Wines

Wine: Sauvignon Blanc, Pinot Grigio, Albarino, Gruner V.

Food: Green Veggies, Roasted Veggies, Carbs, Fish

Sweet Wines

Wine: Riesling, Chenin Blanc, Moscato

Food: Soft Cheese, Carbs, Cured & Smoked Meat, Dessert

Rich White Wines

Wine: Chardonnay, Oaked Whites, Viognier

Food: Roasted Veggies, Carbs, Rich Fish, White Meat

Sparkling Wines

Wine: Champagne, Franciacorta, Prosecco, Cava

Food: Green Veggies, Soft Cheese, Hard Cheese, Carbs, Fish

Light Red Wines

Wine: Pinot Noir, Grenache, Pinotage, Gamay

Food: Hard Cheese, Carbs, Rich Fish, White Meat

Medium Red Wines

Wine: Sangiovese, Merlot, Cabernet Franc, Tempranillo

Food: Hard Cheese, Carbs, White Meat, Red Meat, Cured & Smoked Meat

Big Red Wines

Wine: Cabernet Sauvignon, Shiraz/Syrah, Zinfandel, Mourvedre, Aglianico

Food: Hard Cheese, Red Meat, Cured & Smoked Meat

Dessert Wines

Wine: Port & Tawny Port, Sherry, Late Harvest, Tokaji

Food: Soft Cheese, Carbs, Cured & Smoked Meat, Dessert

Examples of Pairings

This list is a comprehensive listing of well-known wine and food pairings that are used all over the world. These are broken down by wine type to better serve your needs with specific foods that you can serve as a meal.

Red Wine Pairings

Food, Wine

Pork Chops, Pinot Noir

Demi-Glace, Oregon Pinot Noir

Wild Rice Salad with Mushrooms, Cabernet Franc

Duck Breast w/ Caramelized Apples, Red Burgundy

Lamb Shanks with Olives, Beaujolais

Portobello and Red Pepper Burgers, Carneros Pinot Noir

Grilled Salmon with Olive Butter and Orzo, Russian River Valley Pinot Noir

Lamb with Apricots, Saint-Joseph

Spicy Grilled Shrimp Stew, Mencia

Moussaka, Agiorgitiko

Roasted Asparagus with Aceto Balsamico, Chianti Classico

Steak Frites, Sonoma Zinfandel

Penne with Bacon, Swiss Chard, Jack Cheese and Pecans, Washington Syrah

Roasted Duckling with Merlot-Chocolate Sauce and Roasted Beets, Long Island Merlot

Baked Rigatoni with Eggplant and Sausage, Primitivo

Slow-Cooked Rack of Lamb Napa Valley, Cabernet Sauvignon

Rosé Wine Pairings

Food, Wine

Tomato Salad, Bandol Rosé

Tuna and Egg on a Baguette, Tavel Rosé

Vegetable Soup, Cotes de Provence

Bouillabaisse,   Spanish Rosé

White Wine Pairings

Food,   Wine

Avocado, Tomato and Spinach Crepes, New Zealand Sauvignon Blanc

Mussels Provencal, Chilean Sauvignon Blanc

Chicken Satay Burgers, Australian Chardonnay

Spaghetti with Cockles, Greco di Tufo

Wild Mushroom Soup   , California Sauvignon Blanc

Cucumber Soup, New York Riesling

Vietnamese Steak Salad, Gewurztraminer

Chicken Tostadas, Vouvray

Chicken and Mushroom Paellas, Albarino

Linguine with Shrimp, Scallops and Clams, Tocai Friulano

Pork Loin with Cider-Madeira Sauce, Pinot Blanc

Crispy Artichokes, Soave

Pesto Pasta, Vermentino

Chilled Corn Soup with Crab, Australian Chardonnay

Tomato Gazpacho w/Avocado and Lobster, White Bordeaux

Squash Soup with Basil, White Burgundy

Grilled Whole Snapper and Ratatouille, White Rhone Blend

Conclusion

Congratulations! You have just finished reading *"Wine: Everything About Wine From A-Z — Wine History & Everything About Wine."*

By now you should have a thorough understanding of all things wine! My intention was to provide you with all of the information that you need to become a wine expert. You should now have a solid understanding of the history of wine, how it evolved, and what it has been used for throughout history.

Wine is a staple in today's society for various reasons, from wealth to religion. This book took you through the history of wine consumption and production, talking about its impact and role in various cultures, and leading up to the wines that are produced today and discussing the top wine regions. I hope that you were able to learn more about the production process, the difference in wine grapes, the colors of wine, specific flavors, the cost, and what it takes to become a wine taster. The ability to read and understand wine labels is very important when you are attempting to pick the wines that you want to purchase and this book taught you some of the different pieces of information that might be provided on wine labels and what those different items mean to you in terms of quality and taste.

Learning to enjoy wine is a process and it will take time for you to learn the different flavors and smells, but once you do you will be able to enjoy it thoroughly. Chapter 8 of this book provided a thorough explanation of the wine tasting process, including what information should be obtained from wine tasting, how to go about carrying out the wine tasting, and how to use the information that you have obtained. It also discussed some of the options that you can pursue if you are really interested in wine tasting and would like to improve your own skills. Use Chapter 8 again in the future as you become a more efficient wine taster. Once again, it is an art that takes time to learn, but it is fun and enjoyable. I recommend that you try some of the food pairings in Chapter 9: that chapter provides a general idea of the best ways in which to pair wines, as well as more specific suggestions for meals that can be served with many of the wines that you learned about in this book. To get the full benefit of wine, you need to learn to enjoy it with food, and Chapter 9 is a great guide for learning how to do that.

Finally, thank you again for downloading this book. I hope it was useful and you were able to learn something new. If you enjoyed it, I would appreciate it if you would leave a review on Amazon.

Rutherford Winn

Made in the USA
Middletown, DE
10 January 2017